Area and Administration

James W. Fesler

With an Introduction by
Donald F. Kettl

The University of Alabama Press
Tuscaloosa

To the memory of

my father

Whose life was dedicated

to the public service

CONTENTS

PREFACE

This volume consists of lectures delivered at the University of Alabama during the week of December 1 to 6, 1947, as a part of the Southern Regional Training Program in Public Administration. I value highly the opportunity to share in this significant regional program. During my week at Tuscaloosa I found ample confirmation of my impression from afar that Dr. Roscoe C. Martin and his associates in the Bureau of Public Administration and Department of Political Science have succeeded in shaping a fresh approach to the pressing problems of government in the South.

It is remarkable perhaps that when I left after so few days, I felt that I was pulling up roots—so fully had the staff members and students treated me as one of them. I came away with deep respect and affection for the fellows in the training program: Catherine Fox, Burton Friedman, Leon Joyner, Robert MacMillan, Hope Marshall, Buford McRae, Paul Rilling, and Mary Shadow. To my respect for their teachers and counsellors I must add sincere gratitude for a generous hospitality that demonstrated the continuing vitality of the Deep South's best traditions.

These lectures traverse familiar ground. Their function is to place problems of government and administration in an areal framework that is too often ignored. A vast literature has grown up about each of these problems. Federalism, urbanism, fiscal affairs, legislative apportionment, and administrative decentralization are all subjects of range and depth. I have been able to touch on these and like topics only enough to suggest their areal setting. By way of acknowledgment of my debt to scholars who have explored these subjects with insight I have been unable to do more than bring to students' attention the general works that serve as gateways to the specialized literature on each topic. In sum, I shall be content if these lectures lead students to see that administration is rooted in the earth and to explore deeply the areal problems of administration that are merely suggested in these pages.

Chapel Hill
May 1948   JAMES W. FESLER

INTRODUCTION
Donald F. Kettl

This fresh publication of James W. Fesler's classic could scarcely be timelier. He helps us rediscover one of the truly enduring puzzles of public administration. We tend, he writes, to organize government programs by function, such as defense, environmental protection, and transportation. To make the programs work effectively, however, we must translate these functions into actions that work in particular areas, like states, regions, counties, and cities. As Fesler unpacks the puzzle in this trenchant analysis, he reminds us just how central the issue is and how fresh his analysis remains sixty years after this book first appeared. His big question lies at the core of homeland security, welfare reform, and the other great emerging issues.

The basic puzzle works like this: We tend to think of problems in functional ways. We want to build better roads, provide job training to underemployed workers, encourage the production of food, defend the country, and promote international trade, among many other things. We tend to organize government through agencies structured along such functional lines, and to make them work, we hire highly specialized experts to work on headquarters staffs. The Department of Transportation has skilled economists and engineers who focus on highway safety and air traffic control. The EPA has professionals focused on air, water, and soil pollution. The Bureau of Alcohol, Tobacco, Firearms, and Explosives employs some of the world's best experts on arson. However, this expertise is meaningless unless professionals can translate what they know to what can work on the front lines. No two highways, ecosystems, or fires are the same. Applying the same functional approach to all problems will only produce clumsy management; careful management requires administrators to adapt their programs to the widely differing circumstances around the country. Citizens do not live within narrow functions but in a particular place. Government works only to the degree that its different functions come together in a coordinated way to make life in that place better.

Fesler tells us that at the highest policy levels, we tend to specialize by function and generalize by area. At the lowest operating levels, we need specialization by area and generalization by function. Managing that connection is one of government's most important and lasting problems. Fesler's careful look at this problem in *Area and Administration* is just as important now as it was when the book first appeared. It is, at once, a fresh way of reframing the lasting puzzles of centralization and decentralization, and of the struggle to balance administrative efficiency with political responsiveness. It is, Fesler reminds us, the challenge of managing the intersection of the vertical dimensions of government programs with the horizontal dimensions of coordinating them. How do we weave the different threads of government together so that citizens get the government they want?

This puzzle has two especially important dimensions, as Fesler explains in this book. One dimension is federalism. Fesler was among the very first to weave together the political traditions of American intergovernmental relations and its administrative realities. State and local governments are not only entities that define local political life. They are also where the aspirations of American government find their results—or fail to work. As governmental programs have become more ambitious, state and local governments have become more important players in a complex intergovernmental ballet. That has put them on the front lines of translating functional programs to area-based results. As this role has become more important, Fesler's analysis has become more prescient.

The other dimension is field administration. Fesler's work remains public administration's touchstone in understanding how government agencies coordinate their work between headquarters and the field. In recent decades, this problem has received little attention from scholars and even from top executives charged with managing their agencies. However, nearly 90 percent of all federal employees work outside the Washington area. How well government programs work depends, as Fesler suggests, on how well central managers coordinate the work of their field staff. If it has received less attention, it is scarcely because it has become less important. In fact, its importance has only increased as the need for greater coordination of government programs has soared.

This book grew out of lectures that Fesler delivered as part of the famous University of Alabama series on public administration. He had just completed work in Washington during World War II, where he worked for the War Production Board and served as its historian. Along with a host of leading figures in public administration, he contributed to the intellectual capital that helped create the stunningly successful war effort. It was a generation of scholars who had come of age during the New Deal, as government's reach vastly expanded and the demand for skilled management strategies grew as never before in American history. Having built their intellectual capital on domestic policy, they shifted to the vastly difficult task of ramping up the production and logistics operations required to fight a two-front world war. Within months, America moved from a reluctant player in global affairs to a major player in global conflict. It took the best of American public administration, including Jim Fesler, to make it happen.

After the war, this uncommon group of scholars returned to their academic lives. The two Hoover Commissions worked to modernize American government to meet the growing ambitions of a world power that sought great domestic goals as well. The World War II public administrationists supported the commission's work. They turned as well to the search for the truly deep and lasting questions of public administration. Some critics questioned their quest for principles. Others criticized their lack of clear prescriptions. Yet others complained that their work was not in the spirit of the behavioral revolution sweeping the social sciences.

The University of Alabama series brought the field's best thinkers to the university for annual lectures exploring public administration's big questions. It was an all-star lineup that included Arthur Macmahon, Dwithg Waldo, Paul Appleby, John Gauss, Emmette Redford, Roscoe Martin, and Marhsall Dimock. This generation of scholars, whose thinking was seared by the tough experiences of the Depression and World War II, forged a new generation of ideas about public administration. These ideas, in turn, built the intellectual foundation of the modern American administrative state.

By the early 1960s, the field was beginning to drift away from its work, in part because of the rising popularity of new behavioral methodologies and in part because of the growing popularity of public policy, which rose up in opposition to what was often derisively labeled "traditional public administration." The work of this generation of public administrationists, however, has surprisingly withstood the test of time. It is true that they focused on the broad principles. Indeed, a careful reading of *Area and Administration* shows a much greater taste for questions than answers—but it was Fesler's skill in identifying the central and enduring questions that has helped the book endure. Fesler's questions flow not from the emerging techniques of statistical analysis but from the richly textured authority that came from his pre-war staff work for the Brownlow Committee, which helped create the modern office of the presidency, and also from his wartime Washington work. His Alabama lectures reflect the core of Fesler's personal style: crisp analysis that frames big and inescapable questions, answers that are less an effort to prescribe than to block dangerous roads and point in the most useful directions, and an unavoidable taste for the occasional delicious pun.

With uncanny vision, Fesler's *Area and Administration* presents perhaps the foremost examination of the connection between big ideas at the top and the effort to execute them at the bottom. He frames the big questions of federalism in a way that remains powerful today. And he reminds his readers of the importance of issues, including field administration, which analysts often forget. Few works of the era's emerging competing behavioral tradition have endured as well.

In the few places in the book where time has rolled past the analysis, like the look at special governmental organizations such as the Tennessee Valley Authority, the basic issues remain. The TVA does not occupy the same central place in political analysis as it did in the 1940s, but no pattern of government has grown faster since than special district governments, from water and sewer authorities to planning districts. So a careful look past the TVA to the issues with which these special districts must reckon with—a unique strategy of linking area and function—reinforces the power of Fesler's vision.

At the core of the book is a thread that might surprise some readers accustomed to thinking that the post-war scholars struggled to separate politics from administration. Politics runs throughout Fesler's book as the core theme. In fact, it frames his basic question: how top government officials, who create functionally organized programs, can connect with citizens at the grass roots who insist that these programs come together in a coordinated fashion in the places where they live. Politics and the role of administrators in embodying the political life of the government infuse every page.

On one level, therefore, *Area and Administration* is a powerful work of intellectual history. It richly illustrates how the Great Depression and World War II shaped the thinking of scholars who helped build modern American government. But it is also an authoritative work of uncommon insight. The challenges of linking the center with the front lines, of securing vertical and horizontal coordination, and of connecting area and function, have only become more important in twenty-first-century government. Fesler's path-breaking book thus provides an extraordinarily useful foundation for grappling with issues that have become even more important for governance.

Area and
Administration

I: THE PROBLEM OF ADMINISTRATIVE AREAS

Distribution of governmental authority is one of the oldest and most abiding problems of society. By our solutions of this distributive problem we determine whether the government will be stable or unstable; whether it will be dictatorship, a government by and for the few, or a government by and for the many; whether the government will be quickly responsive or unduly laggard in meeting the needs of society; whether policies will be made by popular representatives, by experts, or by an effective combination of the two; whether we shall have the rule of law, the rule of men, or the rule of men under law. It has been traditional since Aristotle to think of this problem primarily in terms of the distribution of functions among the officials at the capital city of a defined geographical area.

There is another phase of the problem on which the experience of Greek city-states casts little light. This is the distribution of governmental authority by area. The dramatic expansion of the scope of governmental activity has strained the traditional patterns of areal distribution of authority. These patterns, therefore, call for reassessment with a view to improving efficiency in the discharge of individual governmental functions, assuring effective coördination of these functions in each area within which men live and work and play, and reinvigorating popular control of both elected and appointed government officials.

Area is a geographic, as well as an administrative, concept. When we speak of the administrative problem of area, therefore, we must not visualize the country as a flat, monotonous plane to be neatly cut into rectangles by a governmental Paul Bunyan armed with a giant cookie cutter. Rather we must see mountain ranges and great river systems, the tobacco and cotton regions of the South, the cut-over forest lands and iron ore pits of the upper Great Lakes, the factory smokestacks of the industrial East, the ships and quays of the seaboard, the oceans of corn and wheat of the land-bound Mid-West, the great grazing country of the prairies, the orchards and forests of the Pacific States. We must see the open country of rural America and what New England signposts call "populated places," some of them so small as to be but tiny villages, some of them so great as to have added the vertical dimension of skyscrapers to the horizontal dimensions by which we usually measure area.

We must be aware, too, of the variety of bases for definition of areas—the dictates of nature in soil, climate, and contour; the commercial and industrial groupings in which man's economic activities are pursued; the cultural unities fixed by historical patterns of migration, shared experience, and customs; the modern communities of settlement that spill over town and city boundaries as if they were not there. Using any one of these bases, it is possible to develop a reasonably defensible division of the country into mutually exclusive areas. Such a division, oriented entirely to a single factor, will coincide with few if any of the divisions developed from application of another factor. We cannot draw a map of drainage basins of the United States and at the same time get both sides of a mountain range into one of the basin areas. We cannot develop identity between Atlanta's commercial trading area and the peach-growing area of the South. The area drawn to reflect homogeneity of economic activity clashes directly with the area drawn to embrace economic heterogeneity and so to approach areal self-sufficiency.

Despite these difficulties, *composite* areas based on a *multiplicity* of factors have been defined by regionalists. The most notable of these efforts are those of Howard W. Odum and of the National Resources Committee's Technical Committee on Regional Planning.[1] Inevitably, the regionalists have had to make initial hypotheses about the optimum number and size of regions, to make major choices between land-use patterns and social culture patterns, to weight the many factors and indices of regionality, and in the end to muster Procrustean daring in slicing off bothersome projections of single-factor natural areas beyond the presumed composite region. This is not to deny the substance behind the popular concept of a New England, a South, or a Middle West. Nor is it to

[1] Howard W. Odum, *Southern Regions of the United States* (Chapel Hill: University of North Carolina Press, 1936); Howard W. Odum and Harry Estill Moore, *American Regionalism* (New York: Henry Holt and Company, 1938); U. S. National Resources Committee, *Regional Factors in National Planning and Development* (Washington: U. S. Government Printing Office, 1935).

deny the need for composite areas for many purposes, a subject to which we shall have occasion to recur. It is important, though, to appreciate the difficulty of drafting a set of composite, multiple-factor areas, and to recognize that sets of such areas drafted by different persons, even though each be thoroughly scientific in approach, will seldom agree.

Whether we are dealing with single-factor or multiple-factor division of the country, it will be well to recognize that the *boundaries* of most types of areas are largely artificial,[2] while the *hearts* of areas are real. As you travel in the country you will not see a clear point at which tobacco culture ends and cotton culture begins. Nor in the statistics of trade will you find that Nashville, Knoxville, and Chattanooga have somehow worked out a clearcut division of the eastern half of Tennessee so that there is no overlap of trade influence on the town and farm population in that area. Instead, the extremities of areas are fringes of culture and influence that interlace, forming a disputed zone rather than a sharp boundary. Moving inward from those borderland zones, however, will be found in each area a core where the expressions of a particular factor or set of factors are so intense as to establish a clear distinction from the cores of other areas.

The division of the country into single-factor areas or into composite regions generally assumes the importance of contiguity of areas and comprehensive alloca-

---

[2] An exception would have to be made for such natural areas as drainage basins whose bounds can readily be ascertained by following streams to their sources.

tion of all the land surface of the country. In our approach to areal aspects of administration, it will be useful to note also the existence of *island areas,* each surrounded by relatively unrelated territory for the purpose in hand, and each having important similarities to other island areas. Great metropolitan centers of population, for instance, have perhaps more social, economic, and governmental problems in common with one another than they have in common with their hinterlands. The steel production areas centering about Pittsburgh, Gary, and Birmingham can for some purposes be treated together as a unity better than they can be treated as parts of the industrial East, the breadbasket Middle West, and the cotton-tobacco South.

Finally, we must bring to the forefront a consideration that has been implicit in what has already been said. The concept of area involves no particular assumption about magnitude of area. The nation itself is an area. And if the nation be divided into the six regions of Odum or the twelve regions of the National Resources Committee, the concept of area may be further pursued to produce sub-regions and sub-sub-regions. We may talk of the area of the South, and, as readily, of the Tennessee Valley area, the Savannah wholesale grocery area, and the slum area of a particular city.

2

It is with this background of natural areal groupings of men and their conditioning environments that we must turn to the administrative problem of area. Through government, a luxuriant growth of administrative areas has taken place on top of the natural areas we have examined. Sometimes these administrative areas have been designed to match the natural areas; sometimes they have been deliberately fashioned to choke the expression of natural groupings; as often as not their delineation has taken place without regard to the relevance of such groupings.

Administrative areas have been of three major types, which we shall call the general governmental area, the special or limited-purpose governmental area, and the field service area. The first two types, which have in common a broad governmental characteristic, as distinct from the narrowly administrative, are the areas that mark out the territorial jurisdictions of units of government. William Anderson has defined a unit of government as "a resident population occupying a defined area that has a legally authorized organization and governing body, a separate legal identity, the power to provide certain public or governmental services, and a substantial degree of autonomy including legal and actual power to raise at least a part of its own revenue."[3]

Of the over 155,000 such units of government in the United States, about 38,000 may be treated as fitting our category of general governmental areas, and about 117,-000 as corresponding to the special or limited-purpose governmental area.[4] The general governmental areas serve the governments of the nation, the states, counties

[3] William Anderson, *The Units of Government in the United States* (Chicago: Public Administration Service, new ed., 1942 and 1945), p. 10.

[4] The figures are based on Bureau of the Census, U. S. Department of Commerce, *Governmental Units in the United States: 1942* (Washington: U. S. Government Printing Office, 1944).

and parishes, cities, villages, and other incorporated places, and towns and townships in the New England and Congressional land-survey sense. The special governmental areas are illustrated by school districts, road and bridge districts, drainage districts, irrigation and conservation districts, soil conservation districts, and housing authorities. Despite the obvious *ad hoc* character of such areas, each serves a separate governmental entity having substantial autonomy in performance of service and in raising of at least part of its revenue.

Our third category, the field service area, is autonomous neither in function nor in financial support. Field service areas are established for the convenient execution of the duties of an administrative part of a unit of government. Any administrative agency having other than purely research responsibilities must carry its work from the center where the agency's top officials are located— Washington, the state capital, or the town hall—to the people in their homes and places of work. This is done through field officials specialized as to area responsibilities. The policeman on his beat and the fire station with its district are familiar examples at the local level. Highway districts, agricultural extension districts, and factory inspection districts are illustrative of state field service areas. In 1943 a tabulation disclosed that Federal agencies had over 140 different *sets* of field service areas, of which the Federal Reserve Districts, Social Security Administration Regions, Customs Districts, and General Land Office Districts are among the most familiar. Each of the large field service areas can be and often is further divided into sub-areas and sub-sub-areas, with the result that a Federal agency may carry on its field work through a hierarchy of areas ranging from as small an area as a county or town up to as large an area as the Southern region. We have no tabulation of the number of field service areas such as the Bureau of the Census provides for governmental areas. But the number would be startling.

The identification of general governmental areas, special governmental areas, and field service areas far from exhausts the areal arrangements for the functioning of government. We are passing by election districts, ranging from states and congressional districts down to wards and precincts, and involving the fascinating technique of gerrymandering. Similarly, judicial districts will receive no consideration here. Nor can we give attention to those less formally defined areas that provide the bases for regional or sectional blocs in Congress focussed on the welfare of the silver mines, the cattle industry, or the cotton farmers, or centered in an isolationist foreign policy or a St. Lawrence waterway. It is with administrative areas that we shall be primarily concerned.

3

Now, with some understanding of the existence and character of natural areas and administrative areas, what are the kinds of problems that demand our attention? At this early stage in our joint exploration, it will be desirable to consider what I have called governmental areas separately from field service areas, although later we shall have to look at both types simultaneously so as to discover the interplay that takes place or should take place between the two. Among governmental areas there are vertical distributions of authority and horizontal distributions of authority. The vertical distribution is often conceived of in legalistic terms. The relation between Washington and the state capitals is called federal, and the United States Constitution with its judicial gloss provides the legal source for understanding of this federal system. The dangerous formalism of the strictly legal approach is perhaps best illuminated when we turn to the vertical distribution of authority between states and local governments. This relation, like that existing within foreign non-federal nations, is called unitary. By this is meant the formal lodging of all authority with the central government—the state—and the complete dependence of local governments on gracious grants of at least temporary power from the state. Whereas in federal governments the vertical distribution of authority is settled by a constitution, in a unitary government this distribution is in large part settled by acts of the central government's legislature. From a less formal standpoint, though, it must be recognized that in a unitary government as in a federal government all functions cannot be performed at the center. Power, however limited, and however much subject to recall, must be devolved on counties, cities, towns, and special districts. The vertical distribution of authority between the nation and the states and between the states and their local governments is therefore a problem all of one piece.

The questions growing out of the vertical distribution of authority can be appreciated only from what I call, with no disrespect, the worm's eye or under-all view of the ordinary citizen. We are accustomed to phrase the problem as if the national government is the unity, from which lines fan out to 48 state governments, from each of which in turn lines diverge to hundreds or thousands of counties, cities, towns, and special districts. Instead of this theistic view, with government as the god-center of the universe, the humanistic view starts with the individual citizen as the point from which to gain sound perspective. It is on him that all governmental activities converge. Unless they make sense at the point of convergence, no mechanical harmony at each of the governmental centers from which these impulses originate can be accepted as an index of sound statecraft.

From his under-all position the citizen looks upward through the many layers of government that minister to his needs, regulate his freedom of action, and demand his financial support. Unless he is in a rural area, he is a citizen of a town or city, a county, a state, and the nation—four levels of general government. In addition, he can hardly avoid falling within a school district that, independently of the general governments, educates his children and obtains some of his money for taxes. Quite possibly, especially in rural areas, he will also be within the jurisdiction of two or more other types of special districts.

What does this citizen ask for in this complex of governments? Certainly, that functions wholly allocated to one or another layer shall be so allocated as to be efficiently performed, cost the least money per unit of service, and be subject to effective democratic control by himself and his fellow-citizens; that in the case of functions shared by two or more layers of government there shall be adequate methods of collaboration between such layers; that the multiple-layer system shall not be so canonized and further complicated as to elude his comprehension, for without such comprehension democratic control languishes; that layers of government whose areas have ceased to be adequate for their original functions shall either be abolished outright or be expanded or contracted to more appropriate dimensions. These are not unreasonable demands. How well American government has met them will be a subject for our later examination.

The *horizontal* distribution of authority among governmental areas poses a different sort of problem. Here the basic fact is the comprehensive division of a land area—the world, a nation, or a state—into mutually exclusive areas controlled by coördinate governments at the same layer of the vertical hierarchy of governments. The legal areas of particular governments seldom coincide with or wholly embrace the natural areas defined by the problems with which society must deal. In the majority of cases the governmental areas have been laid out with a surveyor's rod or a politician's astuteness rather than with an eye to the matching of natural areas. Consequently, the ordinary pressures of day-to-day government force us to devise methods of dealing with great rivers flowing through many states, with criminals fleeing across city, county, state, and even national jurisdictions, and with disease germs spreading their scourge without deference to man-made boundaries. In some cases the obvious avenue of solution is the enlargement of existing governmental areas. Other cases may require the transfer of responsibility for a function from many small governmental areas to the next higher layer of government, whose greater area will approach more nearly the area marked out by the problem to be attacked. Where these solutions are not appropriate or practically attainable, emphasis must be shifted to devising effective means of international, interstate, intercounty, and intermunicipal coöperation.

While the distinction between vertical and horizontal distribution of authority is useful for orderly consideration of the welter of issues in the areal phase of governmental operation, it should not blind us to the need for welding the two for a complete picture. On many problems we need not just effective vertical coöperation or horizontal coöperation. An interstate compact requires both the agreement of several states and the sanction of the Federal government. The laying out of a highway system needs joint vertical action among all layers of government and horizontal coöperation among contiguous states, counties, and municipalities.

From this preliminary exploration of general governmental and special governmental areas, we turn to a brief examination of field service areas. It will be recalled that these are areas marked out as the territorial jurisdictions of field service employees of particular administrative agencies. They have more kinship, then, with the single-factor natural areas and the special-purpose governmental areas than they have with composite natural areas and general governmental areas. Being tied to particular functions, not every field service area within which a citizen lives has a high degree of significance to him. The ordinary citizen has little concern with lighthouse districts, with census divisions, or with vocational education regions. On the other hand, he will usually feel some interest in his internal revenue district, Federal Reserve district, Federal Housing Administration district, and Federal Bureau of Investigation field division; for it is through such areas and their headquarters-cities that he will pay his income taxes, change the beneficiary of his Government bonds, get his house plans approved for mortgage insurance, and initiate the apprehension of violators of many Federal laws.

With all this diversity of interest and non-interest, the ordinary citizen nonetheless has a stake in the construction of field service areas by a government. He wants efficiency and economy in the field administration of individual functions; ultimate responsibility of field officials to the people, through the administrative hierarchy leading to the central government with its elected chief executive and legislators; responsiveness to local opinion through consultation with citizens living in the field service areas; and, finally, and most difficultly, coördination of the many functional field services operating in the same natural area.

These considerations will lead us into an analysis of the drafting of field service area boundaries and of the factors that need attention to bring such boundaries into reasonable harmony with natural areas, to limit the span of control of central and field officials, to save travel and communication expense for officials and for citizens, and to facilitate decentralization and coördination.

Again we encounter not only problems of areal

bounding, but also problems of vertical and horizontal relations. These are posed, though, in a somewhat different setting than are similar relations of general governmental areas. For each function administered through an agency field service there needs to be a distribution of authority among the central office, the field areas, and the sub-areas. Lines of vertical communication need to be strung up for commands, inquiries, appeals, and advice. Many other issues, often both intriguing and perplexing, need settlement in terms of vertical relations within the single agency.

Horizontal problems are presented in quite a different form from the inter-area coöperation that is so significant for governmental areas. Here, our concern is with a common area in which many agencies of the same government have field agents at work. The emphasis in individual governments upon functional distribution of authority among administrative agencies means that the strongest, and to a remarkable extent the only, line of relationship of a field agent is vertical. With his eyes so strongly developed for looking upward and downward, the muscles that would turn his eyes to the right and to the left tend to atrophy. He may not know, therefore, what other field agents are active in the area, what they are doing, how their work impinges on his, and what can be done to assure coördination of the government's work in the single area.

What we have said of natural areas, general and special governmental areas, and field service areas reveals what will become the recurrent theme of these lectures. The theme is the reciprocal adjustment of function and area. By function is meant the conserving of soil, the settlement of labor disputes, the quenching of fires, the harnessing of waterpower, the carrying of the mail, the collection of taxes and fees, and all the myriad activities with which modern administration is charged. By area we mean the ordinary citizen's ambit as he moves about from home to his work and his play, and the physical, social, and economic areas dictated by the location and movement of phenomena with which social action is concerned. The administrative adjustment of function and area may occur in either of two ways. One is to consider each function separately, identify the single-factor areas best adapted to that function, and make the administrative areas for the function conform to the single-factor areas. The other is to start with emphasis on the interrelation of functions and the need for coördinated administration and area-based popular control of those functions as they affect a given community or group of communities. Here, then, the need is for identifying the best multiple-factor areas for a composite of functions, sacrificing perfect adjustment of area to the individual functions but trying to reduce the degree of sacrifice as much as possible. In a sense, we are faced by a choice of adjusting area to function or adjusting function to area. To avoid being immobilized on the horns of this dilemma, we are forced to develop practical compromises. This task is not an academic exercise, for it is the ordinary citizens, you and I, whose ox is being gored.

One easy compromise is always at hand. Some fear that fitting single-factor functional areas into composite governmental areas is too much like trying to fit square pegs into round holes. In fact, of course, the latter task is not impossible if the diagonal measurement of the square peg is less than the diameter of the round hole. Though geometricians cannot square the circle, we can at least circle the square. We can, then, encompass single-factor areas in composite governmental areas if the latter are large enough. The implication is clear: that reasonably satisfactory areas for individual functions can be attained without sacrifice of coördination among functions if we are willing to dispense with our present smaller governmental areas. What, if any, democratic values we may thereby lose we shall have to reserve for later examination.

4

We have so far avoided use of the words "centralization" and "decentralization." The terms are so familiar that we need not tarry over them in this introductory effort to develop a vocabulary that will enable us to attach individual areal problems to their proper genus and species. It will suffice here to make one important distinction. The devolution of authority can take place either along *functional* lines at the center or along *areal* lines emphasizing the usefulness of governmental and field service areas. Suppose, for instance, that the nation has the task of encouraging the settlement of labor disputes. A national board is created, which is simple enough; but beyond that lie perplexing problems of devolution since the board of, say, five men cannot itself handle the volume of business or bring the requisite familiarity with technical and local background to the wide range of cases. One solution is to encourage the states to establish boards to handle labor disputes arising within their jurisdictions, with the national board concentrating on truly national disputes. This involves devolution to governmental areas, the states.[5] Another solution is for the national board to establish its own regional offices to which all disputes arising in the regions will first come, with only appeals being taken to the national board. This is devolution by field service areas.

Both of these methods, devolution by governmental area and devolution by field service area, fit within the earlier analysis. There is, though, a third solution. The national board may establish in Washington sub-boards or divisions, each specializing on a particular industry. Thus, there might be a unit for the steel industry, one for the coal industry, one for the textile industry, and so on.[6] A variant of this solution is for the national board to set up a large technical staff at Washington, with a wage division, hours-of-labor division, working-conditions division, employee-polling division, unfair-practices division, and so on. In theory at least, such a set of divisions could process the issues in a dispute, bringing to bear a fa-

[5] I am assuming, for purposes of illustration, that there is no constitutional obstacle to the national board's being vested with the powers which it or Congress elects to devolve on or leave with the state boards.

[6] The National Recovery Administration's code authorites are the most extreme examples of this approach, for in effect the devolution was to the higher command of individual industries rather than to government officials. A major dispute of war administration was over the question whether the NRA pattern, which left the public interest poorly protected, should be repeated in industrial mobilization. On this, see Edythe W. First, *Industry and Labor Advisory Committees in the National Defense Advisory Commission and the Office of Production Management* (Washington: Civilian Production Administration, 1946).

miliarity with settlement of these issues in comparable disputes in other industries and factories, and arming the national board members with sufficient information and recommendations to speed up the board's handling of cases. Because of the size of staff required for such an approach, the same range of expertness could not readily be reproduced through the staffs of state labor dispute boards or through the staffs of regional units of the national board.

In almost any governmental activity there is a choice as to the method of farming out the work from the top administrator's office. True, the issue is not always an either-or proposition. Authority can be devolved both along functional lines and along areal lines. But even where this option exists, an emphasis, conscious or unconscious, is usually made upon one or the other of these methods. Because appropriations and personnel for an activity are limited, it is often necessary to decide whether to allot most of those resources to a strong, functionalized central office on the one hand or to a strong areally organized field service or set of state agencies operating under grants-in-aid on the other. You cannot have your cake and eat it too.

5

Let us see where we stand in the analysis of the problem of administrative areas. First, we have prefaced our attack on the areal distribution of governmental authority by an effort to see area as a geographic, social, and economic reality. Such "natural areas," we have discovered, can be identified either by using a single factor, such as soil type, or by applying a multiplicity of factors so as to produce composite areas. In either event, the centers of areas, where the relevant phenomena are spotted so thickly as to create an umbral black splotch, are more readily agreed upon than the boundaries that must somehow be drawn in the penumbral zones where the phenomena occur less frequently. In some cases, furthermore, phenomena are concentrated in a few locales instead of being distributed over the land surface of the country, and we therefore recognize island areas. Finally, "natural area" was seen to be a neutral term that begs no question as to the appropriate magnitude of area.

Next, we identified three kinds of administrative area: the general governmental area like the state or city, the special or limited-purpose governmental area like the school district, and the field service area like the Social Security Administration Region. It was proposed that among the general and special governmental areas we distinguish the vertical distribution of authority from the horizontal distribution of authority. In the case of the former, we tried to visualize the ordinary citizen operating under four or more layers of governmental areas, and we tried to find out what this citizen might reasonably expect of this complex structure. The horizontal distribution of authority among coördinate governments, each of which administers a roughly similar type of area, brought us to the need for matching governmental areas with the natural areas defined by the phenomena subject to such governments' control. A complementary c alternative need was that for horizontal intergoverı mental coöperation.

Field service areas, it was found, involve us in problems of adaptation of such areas to natural areas and to administrative considerations, development of vertical communication between the central agency and its field agents, and coördination of all of the central government's field agents operating in the same general area.

Finally, we established the theme of reciprocal adjustment of function and area, and qualified the emphasis of these lectures on areal devolution of authority by noting the alternative of functional devolution to industry units or to technically specialized groups of civil servants.

II: GOVERNMENTAL AREAS

Intergovernmental relations are central to our understanding of the areal aspects of administration.[1] The abundance of literature on the subject makes a descriptive account unnecessary and a prescriptive analysis hazardous. I fear to tread where the angels of the social sciences have already stamped the subject to a pulp. In the brief space of time for our exploration of this exceedingly complex subject we can try to do only three things: To emphasize that intergovernmental relations are an areal problem of administration, and not solely a constitutional, political, or emotional problem; to determine the factors that are relevant to the reciprocal adjustment of governmental functions and governmental

[1] Among the most useful general studies of governmental areas and the problem of intergovernmental relations are the following, to which I am indebted for much of my own orientation in the field: William Anderson, *Federalism and Intergovernmental Relations* (Chicago: Public Administration Service, 1946); George C. S. Benson, *The New Centralization* (New York: Farrar and Rinehart, Inc., 1941); Jane Perry Clark, *The Rise of a New Federalism* (New York: Columbia University Press, 1938); W. Brooke Graves, *Uniform State Action* (Chapel Hill: University of North Carolina Press, 1934); Committee on Intergovernmental Fiscal Relations, U. S. Treasury Department, *Federal, State, and Local Government Fiscal Relations* (78th Cong., 1st Sess., Senate Document 69, 1943); "Intergovernmental Relations in the United States," *Annals of the American Academy of Political and Social Science* 207 (January 1940); V. O. Key, Jr., *The Administration of Federal Grants to States* (Chicago: Public Administration Service, 1937). I have omitted from this note the works that are cited subsequently in this chapter.

areas; and to examine the alternative means of achieving a better adjustment of functions and areas.

In bespeaking a recognition of the *administrative* aspect of intergovernmental relations, I do not discount the other aspects, nor do I ignore the many ways in which they condition the administrative problem. The constitutionally federal basis of Federal-state relations both sets legal bounds to the ready adjustment of function and area and provides a controversial historical setting for a contemporary approach to such adjustment. We are constantly having to weave from the threads of eighteenth-century constitutional phrases the mantle of respectability for a distribution of governmental authority that comports with twentieth century needs.

State-local relations are seriously conditioned by the legal doctrine of state supremacy. The state legislature, the principal beneficiary of this doctrine, is typically dominated by rural or small-town members. They apply their ideas of government and economics gained from experience in rural counties and tiny villages to the complex problems of great cities like Chicago, New York, Atlanta, and Birmingham. Often the legislatures impose a straight-jacket of uniformity on cities and counties, specifying a single method of organizing all local governments, prescribing what officers there must be, and determining which officers shall be elected and which appointed.[2] The state constitution, as well as the

---

[2] Examples of these practices are given in the Sixth Report of the New York State Tax Commission for the Revision of the Tax Laws, *Reorganization of Local Government in New York State* (Albany: J. B. Lyon Co., New York Legislative Document [1935] No. 63), pp. 49-139.

legislature, may be the offender in uniformly hamstring-
ing local governments and stimulating excessive multiplication of general and special local units through re-
strictions on tax rates and incurrence of debt. At the
other extreme the legislature may by special legislation
make decisions for individual cities and counties. In
North Carolina two-thirds of all state laws are special and
local. At one recent session the North Carolina legislature took the trouble to prohibit the catching of oysters
of less than three inches in size in Pamlico County
streams, prohibited public dances on Sundays in Chatham
County, forbade the operation of filling stations in
Northhampton County on Sundays between 10:00 a.m.
and 12:30 p.m., and extended to four years the term of
office of the Register of Deeds of Cherokee County
elected at the preceding general election!

Political as well as constitutional problems compli-
cate intergovernmental relations. Federal-state coöperation is handicapped in states where the dominant party is
different from that of the President. State-local relations
are often bitter when rural-urban enmity in the legislature is fanned by the enmity between rival political parties, one in control of the legislature and the other in control of a city government. Much special legislation has
its roots in political vindictiveness. Politics also throws
obstacles in the way of any revision of governmental areas
that would reduce patronage and force a reorientation of
political machinery.

Emotional attachments condition any adjustment of
function and area. There are emotional loyalties to existing areas that cannot lightly be disturbed. Alabama is

not just an artificially drawn segment of the earth's surface, but a state of mind, an object of affectionate attachment, a complex of history and culture that is unique
among governmental areas. At the local level of emotional loyalty I need merely cite Brooklyn without further comment. Finally, emotional attachment to ideas and
slogans like states' rights, local self-government, and home
rule, and emotional reaction to words like centralization
and bureaucracy illustrate the symbolism with which any
scientific approach to administrative areas must cope.

2

These constitutional, political, and emotional problems provide a setting of which we must take account.
Their existence, however, must not divert us from recog-
nizing that there are also peculiarly administrative factors that bear on the reciprocal adjustment of governmental function and governmental area. The most important of these factors are four.

The first is the need for adjusting governmental areas
to the natural distribution of phenomena with which government must deal. This emphasis on the relation of natural areas to governmental areas has been adequately
explored earlier. I would here simply remind you that
we *can* define the cotton area, the river valley, the urban
settlement area, and the cut-over forest area, and that an
integrated governmental attack on the problems of each
such area is most successful if the attack is under the gen-
eralship of a government whose territorial jurisdiction
embraces the whole of the natural area.

Administrative efficiency is a second factor relevant

to solving the function-area equation. For many governmental functions efficiency requires the development of a staff of officials of diverse skills; otherwise the people are denied the fruits of expertness developed in the specialized channels of education and experience. If the jack-of-all-trades has become as limited in value in government as in our division-of-labor industrial life, the impulse to bigness is as characteristic of government as of industry. A staff of specialists will have an adequate work-load only if it has a large clientele. And a large clientele exists only in the larger governmental areas, the exact size depending on population density and, more especially, on the density of the phenomena with which particular governmental functions are concerned.

Administrative efficiency also sets *limits* to the optimum size of governmental areas. As in industry, bigness can be pressed beyond the point of efficiency. Whether we have yet mastered or can master the complexities of a large bureaucracy is a moot point. The difficulties of such mastery certainly are greater where the skills relevant to a function have become so specialized that their practitioners speak different languages, fail to share a common philosophy, and magnify the importance of their special interests at the expense of a balanced agency program. In other ways, too, administrative efficiency sets bounds to the expansion of governmental areas. The consolidated school with its specialized staff of teachers and complement of equipment dictates a larger area for school districts than was appropriate to the one-room school house of those raised on McGuffey's Readers. But administrative efficiency also requires that these areas be so limited in size as neither to require expensive and unduly lengthy bus transportation of school children nor to destroy community of interest among the pupils.

Administrative efficiency suggests still another consideration: That if there are substantial differences in the *tone* of governments at different levels—by which I mean susceptibility to corruption, profligacy, and spoils—functions should be allotted to the level where administration promises to be least vulnerable to abuse by special interests and political factions.

To consideration of natural areas and administrative efficiency must be added a third factor in the adjustment of governmental area to function: the adequacy of fiscal resources of the area. That there are great variations of fiscal resources among governmental areas has become a commonplace. In 1946 the per capita income of residents of New York State was $1,633, while that of Mississippi residents was $555. For all eleven states of the Southeast the per capita income was only about $800, well below the $1,200 figure for the nation.[3] Within individual states the disparity in taxable resources among the counties and among the cities is often more startling than that among states. Because fiscal resources set limits to governmental service, the unequal distribution of wealth and income results in a checkerboard pattern of functional efficiency among the states and among local areas. Because the South has more than its share of the black areas on such maps, we in the South have a pe-

[3] "State Income Payments in 1946," *Survey of Current Business* (August 1947), pp. 1-16, at p. 14.

culiarly acute awareness of areal differences in fiscal resources and their relation to differences in the functional adequacy of our governments.

For such differences in fiscal resources there are several possible adjustments. Areas so small as to lack a taxable base capable of supporting minimal standards of governmental performance may be enlarged to embrace greater fiscal resources. But no absolute size of area can be predicated. A large area may still be a poor area. Mere expansion of poor governmental areas to include adjoining areas that are equally poor would be no solution. Alternatively, some functions may be shifted to higher levels of government having areas large enough to assure adequate fiscal resources. And a further alternative is to leave the function at the lower governmental level, but have the higher level subsidize the function.

The fourth factor is popular control. This factor means such different things to different people and is so burdened with emotional overtones that it almost defies objective description. We may all agree, however, that government must not be irresponsible, that the channels for popular control must be simple and clear, and that the people's interest in control must be kept vital.

We have, then, four major factors to consider in the adjustment between function and governmental area—namely, natural distribution of phenomena, administrative efficiency, fiscal adequacy, and popular control. No one of these four factors should be the sole touchstone in determining the size and functions of governmental areas. All four must be weighed in relation to each governmental function.

At the same time, the combined weight of these factors when matched against the governmental area pattern inherited from the eighteenth and nineteenth centuries suggests several general conclusions. The inherited pattern rather directly reflects technological, social, and economic conditions of the earlier centuries. Primitive transportation facilities, Jacksonian ideas of administration by amateurs, noninterventionist concepts of government's role, and slight pressure on taxable resources all account for many phases of areal bounding and the distribution of authority among areas. The pattern, being adjusted to such conditions, is weighted in favor of small areas and decentralization of authority. The conditions of our own time exert pressure for enlargement of areas and a greater degree of centralization.

The expanded concept of government's role, because it has developed simultaneously with the centralization trend, is often confused with centralization. Although careful studies are available, we hardly need their evidence to establish that at the same time that the Federal Government has been acquiring functions earlier reserved to the states, the functions of the states have also expanded; and that, similarly, municipal activities are now more extensive than in previous centuries.

Because centralization has had to battle against patterns established earlier, the drama of the contest has led some to the mistaken conclusion that our smaller areas are destined to become empty shells, our local governments and states simply vermiform appendices in the body politic. It is well to have clear that the territorial expanse of a nation as large as the United States requires governmental areas of at least three orders of magnitude. We need a national government covering the total area; we need a group of subnational governments each covering a significant portion of the national area—whether one-forty-eighth or one-sixth or some intermediate fraction we leave for debate; we need a group of municipal governments for the island areas in which many people live closely together and have common problems growing directly from their collective social life; and at the same level, we need for the more sparsely settled areas, governments that cover less ground than the subnational governments and provide services not unlike those of the municipal governments, though modified to meet peculiarly rural and village needs.

There can be no satisfactory adjustment of function and area that is not rooted in the need for vital, healthy democratic government at all three levels—national, subnational, and local, for each level and its corresponding governmental area have unique importance to the citizen who supports and is served by American government. For this reason, though the four factors will be relevant in the determination of the appropriate governmental area for each function, they constitute challenges for each of the units of general government. The people cannot afford a government at any level whose area has no relation to the natural areas of that government's functions, whose administrative standards are low, whose fiscal resources cannot support minimal standards of governmental services, whose officials escape popular control. This approach runs contrary to the advocacy of centralization based on the superior administrative efficiency of central governments because of their recruitment of employees on a basis of merit, their gearing of the executive branch organization to the need for coördination, their capitalization on best administrative procedures. Too, it is a departure from the case for decentralization that rests on the argument that popular control is more effective in small governmental areas. Each level of government is destined to continue to play too important a role for us to deny and so neglect the possibility of administrative efficiency in local governments or for us to deny and so neglect the possibility of popular control of state and national governments.

This leads to a further caution. Our minds are so hospitable to easy generalization that we far too glibly talk about "the states" or about "the local governments" as if they were all of one piece. Legally of course each does belong to a class of governments. But when we start to test them by their relation to natural areas, to administrative efficiency, to fiscal adequacy, or to popular control, the rich variety of the pattern becomes clear. There are states that are smaller than counties in other states; there are states that are larger than many foreign nations. Some states have archaic governmental structures, patronage filling of administrative offices, incompetent administration; others set a very high standard of administrative efficiency. Some states are poor and cannot afford decent educational, welfare, and health services; others can and do finance excellent programs in these fields. Some states are run by special interests and political machines; others have governments that are sensitively attuned to the public interest and fairly judged at the polls. Much the same contrasts are found among cities. Further qualifying quick generalization is the change that can be wrought in a single state or city government. Order can be brought into a disorderly administrative and fiscal system and popular control be reinvigorated simply by a change in political majorities. While one year New York City may be identified as an example of the low quality of city government, the next year under different leadership it may stand forth as a promise of what other cities can aspire to.

Such an approach, however, is difficult to reconcile with the demand that the student of governmental areas either take his stand with the angels chanting the hosannas of states' rights and small local governmental areas, or sell his soul to the Satanic plotters of centralization and enlargement of local areas. Without prejudicing the case for decentralization and retention of diminutive local areas, we may properly inform ourselves concerning the angels' strange bedfellows. Those opposed to effective performance of a regulatory or service function of government often prefer that the natural area of phenomena should be so segmented among governmental areas that no single government can be in command of the situation, the numerous governments involved will frustrate one another, and the special interests in the large natural area can focus their pressures to prevent any of the small-area governments from taking "ill-advised" action. Another group also are suspect as worshippers at the shrine of states' rights and local self-government. These are the officials and special interests of the smaller governmental areas. A major drag on the move for con-

solidation of neighboring counties has been the reluctance of county office-holders and political parties to see
a merging of offices and a reduction in the aggregate
number of officials. Localized special interests account
for interstate trade barriers erected by states to protect
"home industries." Civic clubs and women's organizations recoil from absorption in the groups of a larger
community. To the saboteurs of effective performance
of governmental functions and to the local interests of
office-holders, entrepreneurs, and "joiners" must be added the opponents of a share-the-wealth approach to the
problem of fiscal adequacy. An area that is wealthy pre-
fers both to keep the tax on that wealth low and to have
the flow of expenditures from such tax revenue confined
within the bounds of the area. New York does not like
to have the Federal Government's taxes siphon off New
York money for expenditure in Mississippi. Wealthy
satellite towns do not like to be annexed to cities having
inadequate fiscal resources to support the city government's functions. Not all those who murmur the shib-
boleths of states' rights and local self government are true
Gileadites like David E. Lilienthal and Gordon Clapp.

3

With the factors relevant to the adjustment of area
and function isolated, what techniques are at hand for
effecting the adjustment dictated by these factors? There
are two major approaches. One is completely to redesign governmental areas to fit particular functions or
groups of functions. The other is to accept the present

areal framework and to readjust functional relationships among the existing governmental areas.

The redesigning of governmental areas is an intriguing game. A strong case can be made for the proposition that regional governments should be established, each embracing an area as large as that currently occupied by several states. Many problems, the argument goes, have natural areas larger than states yet smaller than the nation. Under our present system of governmental areas, we have the options only of letting such problems be bungled on a piecemeal basis by the states or of transferring these problems to the jurisdiction of the national government where legislators from areas not directly affected by the problems may swing the deciding votes on regional policies. The fact that many problems elude effective handling by 48 separate governmental areas averaging 62,000 square miles does not mean that they should be turned over to a single national area of 3,000,-000 square miles. An intermediate area is needed, either to supplant or to supplement the state areas.

Such a governmental area, the argument continues, would have greater vitality than the present states. It not only would have a more direct relation to natural problem areas, but its population would have more of a cultural homogeneity and distinctness from other regions than is true of any state population. In a sense, the South is more real than Alabama, the Middle West more real than Kansas, New England more real than Vermont. Part of the weakness of our state governments may stem directly from the fact that historical accidents rather than cultural unities have set their areal boundaries. The revitalization of a subnational level of government may therefore depend on matching subnational governmental areas with the natural problem and cultural regions of the country.

Constitutional obstacles, the fear of a revival of sectionalism, the existence of state loyalties, and sheer inertia all make regional governments an unlikely answer to the need for reciprocally adjusting areas and functions.

There remains the possibility of redesigning areas of local government within the state. This can go forward on either of two fronts. There can be an enlargement of local areas of general governments, an abolition of unnecessary general governmental areas and an absorption of the functions of special governmental areas by the general governments. This may be termed the general approach. In contrast, one can take each function separately and establish the appropriate area for each function, setting up where necessary a specialized unit of government to perform the particular function.

The general approach is illustrated by William Anderson's proposal to reduce the 155,000 units of local government in the United States to about 18,000. For the average state this would mean cutting its number of local units from nearly 3,230 to about 375. Anderson would abolish almost all special districts—among them the 109,000 school districts—absorbing their functions in the general governmental units; he would wipe out the townships of the Middle Western and some Middle Atlantic states, would consolidate many smaller counties, and would merge city and county in the main urban centers.[4]

Other guides to a general redrafting of local government areas are available. Arthur C. Millspaugh has suggested that the minimum service area for purely administrative purposes should contain not less than 25,000 people, that for the purpose of self-financing a county should contain not less than 20,000 residents, and that the area of a local governmental unit should not exceed 6,400 square miles.[5] The Council of State Governments' Committee on State-Local Relations has concluded that "reasonable efficiency is probably unobtainable with [governmental] units of fewer than 25,000 inhabitants, while maximum effectiveness probably requires a population of 50,000." Yet half of the nation's counties have fewer than 25,000 inhabitants and 86 per cent have fewer than the optimum 50,000.[6]

The difficulty with this general approach is that, barring a ground-swell of public sentiment, or the contrivance of a new strategy of action, the experts' recommendations for enlargement and consolidation of areas do not seem to have a chance of adoption. Even such a simple proposal as consolidation of neighboring counties, though repeated by the experts in state after state for the past thirty years, has borne almost no fruit. The only

4 William Anderson, *The Units of Government in the United States* (Chicago: Public Administration Service, new ed., 1942 and 1945), pp. 45-46.

5 Arthur C. Millspaugh, *Local Democracy and Crime Control* (Washington: Brookings Institution, 1936), pp. 80-102.

6 Committee on State-Local Relations, Council of State Governments, *State-Local Relations* (Chicago: Council of State Governments, 1946), p. 202.

two actual consolidations in the country have occurred in Georgia and Tennessee. So obvious a need as the bringing of each metropolitan area under a single metropolitan government has been answered with a roaring vacuum of inaction.[7]

The specialized functional approach to the redesigning of governmental areas moves in the opposite direction from the general reform proposals. Under this approach the first step would be the expert determination of separate optimum areas for public health, education, drainage, public welfare, and so on. These special areas would not necessarily be coincident. Thus, the minimum feasible area for highway construction and maintenance would be several times larger than the minimum feasible area for elementary and secondary education. The second step would be the recognition of school districts, highway districts, health districts, and drainage districts as distinct units of government with revenue-raising and decision-making powers independent of the general governments operating in the same areas.

This avenue of reform, while of possible appeal to experts in each of the functional fields, cannot command the endorsement of political scientists. The multiplica-

---

[7] Metropolitan government is a subject in itself, and therefore has not lent itself to extensive analysis within the framework of these lectures. Its importance, however, warrants the attention of students of area and administration. The following studies will be found valuable: Victor Jones, *Metropolitan Government* (Chicago: University of Chicago Press, 1942); Albert Lepawsky, "Development of Urban Government," in U. S. National Resources Committee, *Urban Government* (Washington: U. S. Government Printing Office, 1939), esp. pp. 27-35; and Charles E. Merriam, Spencer D. Parratt, and Albert Lepawsky, *The Government of the Metropolitan Region of Chicago* (Chicago: University of Chicago Press, 1933).

tion of units of government when the citizen is already confused and his tax burdens poorly coördinated, the freeing of functionally specialized agencies from continuing oversight by a general legislative body and a general executive, and the reduction of the ease of interfunctional coöperation among governmental agencies are results to be expected from the special districts approach and to be deplored by students of government. In fact, a minimum program of areal reform should consist of the absorption of virtually all special governmental units and their districts into the general governments and their areas. Even such a minimum program almost immediately precipitates the fundamental question of the adequacy of the general governments from the standpoint of natural areas, administrative efficiency, fiscal resources, and popular control.

4

The dismal prospect that recommendations of experts for redesigning of general and special governmental areas may continue to go unheeded forces us back on an alternative approach. That is to accept the existing units of government with their stubborn attachment to existing areas, to develop horizontal and vertical relations among these governments and areas, and thus to facilitate the reciprocal adjustment of function and area in the light of the claims of natural areas, administrative efficiency, fiscal adequacy, and popular control.

Horizontal coöperation among coördinate governments is one of the most necessary and, at the same time, one of the most cumbersome, techniques of dealing with problems that affect more than one governmental area. Among the states there has sprouted a rich variety of devices for coöperation. Some are nationwide, involving all 48 states, such as the Council of State Governments, the Governors' Conference, the American Legislators' Association, the National Conference of Commissioners on Uniform State Laws, and the associations of state attorneys general, state health officers, state labor commissioners, and state insurance commissioners. Others are regional like most interstate compacts, the Conference of Southern Governors, and the regional planning commissions. Interstate coöperation may be formal or informal.

Among local governmental areas coöperation follows much the same pattern. Statewide, and even nationwide, leagues of municipalities, associations of municipal finance officers, sheriffs, and county commissioners express the associational impulse and serve to emphasize the common interests of coördinate governmental areas at the local level.

Formal or informal agreements among two or more local governments are numerous. For the South, the studies of Cooper on Alabama, Raisty on Georgia, Satterfield and Urban on Mississippi, and Abbott and Greene on Tennessee are rich in illustrations of intermunicipal and city-county coöperation.[8] Sometimes what

---

[8] Weldon Cooper, *Municipal Government and Administration in Alabama* (University, Ala.: Bureau of Public Administration, 1940); Lloyd B. Raisty, *Municipal Government and Administration in Georgia* (Athens: University of Georgia Press, 1941); M. H. Satterfield and Hugh W. Urban, *Municipl Government and Administration in Mississippi* (Jackson: Mississippi

is involved is the joint construction, under a cost sharing formula, of bridges, airports, or public buildings; sometimes it is the leasing or joint use of costly equipment and services for fire-fighting, police radio broadcasting, hospitalization, and road construction; sometimes it is routine coöperation among neighboring police departments in the apprehension of criminals; sometimes it is joint purchasing to obtain quantity discounts.

Tentative conclusions about horizontal relations among governmental areas may be advanced. First, comprehensive inter-area coöperation, involving all the states in the country, or all the local governments within a state or within the country, does not advance us far in the reciprocal adjustment of area and function. If the natural area of a problem is national in scope, the problem cannot be met by attacking it through 48 areas, each independent of the others; nor is uniform action likely no matter how earnest the plea for coöperation. Our experience with almost 60 years' work of the National Conference of Commissioners on Uniform State Laws, and with the noble effort of the Council of State Governments to reduce interstate trade barriers, are suggestive of the modest fruits to be expected of the large-scale approach to getting coöperative action over a very large natural area. Second, comprehensive inter-area coöperation is often more a method of lobbying against accretion of powers by the next higher level of government than a method of coöperation to promote redrafting of govern-

State Planning Commission, 1940); Lyndon E. Abbott and Lee S. Greene, *Municipal Government and Administration in Tennessee* (Knoxville: Division of University Extension, University of Tennessee, 1939).

mental areas, administrative efficiency, adequate fiscal resources, and popular control in meeting the problems of natural areas. Third, comprehensive inter-area coöperation makes its greatest contribution in two ways: in providing central staff research and educational facilities to strengthen the competence with which the governments at a particular level do their job, so that governmental bankruptcy alone cannot justify the transference of authority to higher levels of government; and in stimulating horizontal coöperation among a limited number of contiguous governmental areas. Fourth, the greatest promise of horizontal coöperation lies in the *ad hoc* bi- or tri-lateral arrangements for settling issues arising in the zone of contention where areas meet and for merging governmental areas for particular functions in order to match natural problem areas and provide greater administrative efficiency. Fifth, even in this limited field of horizontal coöperation, formidable handicaps exist in the difficulties of negotiating inter-area contracts (which often closely resembles the process of international negotiation), the problems of establishing satisfactory cost-sharing formulas, the ease of secession from the union, the reluctance to set up joint administrative authorities with real power, and the puzzle of popular control over such joint authorities.

5

I started our discussion of horizontal relations by saying that horizontal coöperation is one of the most necessary and one of the most cumbersome techniques of dealing with problems that affect more than one gov-

ernmental area. It is the combination of hope and despair about horizontal relations that drives us so often to
shift to higher levels of government the authority for
handling problems for which the next lower levels are inadequate.

The logic of these upward transfers of authority has
in most cases forced the opponents back on the argument
that state and local government must continue to exercise
important functions, however ineffectively, if we are to
preserve popular government in this country. Nonetheless, we are today confronted with soundly-bottomed demands for increased Federal participation in education,
health, and welfare functions; and state governments in
turn have been taking over from the local areas important responsibilities in these functional fields, as well
as in the field of public roads.

It is no longer appropriate, however, to think in terms
of mutually exclusive grants of functions to this or that
level of government. What we have is governmental
sharing of functions. Sometimes the sharing is amicable
and follows a consistent pattern—in which case we can
happily speak of "coöperative government." In other
cases the sharing involves duplication, overlapping, and
conflict. Though not all might agree, I should cite public roads administration as a field of coöperative government and tax administration as a field of competitive
government.

The expanding role of the larger governmental areas
is an honest if tacit recognition of the inability of lesser
areas to embrace the natural problem areas, of their administrative inefficiency, their fiscal inadequacy, or their

escape from popular control. The people, though indoc-
trinated with the values of local government, are insistent
in their demand for results. Democracy, especially as expressed in attachment to local government, has never
been defended as the most efficient form of government—
in the narrow sense of efficiency. Americans have wisely
preferred the assumed imperfections of democracy to the
supposed efficiency of monocratic regimes. But the al-
legedly necessary evil of inefficiency should not be apoth-
eosized into a glowing virtue. Government, like any
provider of goods and services, must yield a product that
satisfies the customer. The movement of functions to
higher levels of government with their greater areas is a
genuine response to the need for customer satisfaction.
Functions move upward in our governmental system only
by the vote of legislators tied closely to local constituencies and local interests.

Larger governmental areas can do much to strengthen
the governments in smaller areas. State legislatures can
remove the strait-jacket of uniform laws controlling local
governments, and, even more important, can remove the
shackles of special local legislation. Higher governments
can establish specialized staffs to advise local areas that
cannot afford such staffs. Such technical services can
range all the way from advice on fiscal problems to state
laboratory services for local health departments. Again,
the states can use their grants-in-aid to bolster the fiscal
resources of local areas. Such grants can also be made
conditional on the local areas' setting their own houses
in order—by improving their budget and accounting sys-

tems, recruiting certain groups of employees by the merit system, and even merging tiny governmental areas either permanently or on an *ad hoc* marriage-of-convenience basis.

A large governmental area can reconcile the conflicting demands for uniformity and diversity by directing its resources to provision of uniform *minimal* standards of governmental services while leaving local areas with superior resources free to exceed the minimum. Thus, the state may make grants-in-aid to local areas for minimal standards of welfare, health, and education services that will be observed throughout the state. But each local area might exceed the minimum in whatever degree local fiscal resources and local opinion permit.

The larger governmental areas are obligated to act decisively in the fields where conflict and competition among lesser governmental areas enable the least progressive and coöperative area to dictate the pace of all areas. It is no accident that before 1935 only one state had dared pass an unemployment insurance law. However widespread the recognition of workers' claims to some measure of economic security, no state could act without discouraging the flow of industry into that state. Florida, by foregoing an inheritance tax, attracted thousands of tax-escaping oldsters from other states—nudged along no doubt by their heirs-presumptive. The state with the laxest divorce law sets the national pattern for unknotting the tie that binds. The state with the most inadequate incorporation law fixes the pattern for corporate business throughout the country. In a depression, the states with the least generous relief grants force the migration of their workers to other states, which must either ban immigration or revise their relief grants downward.

The assumption of an expanded role by the larger governmental areas—big government, if we need a label—parallels the growth of big business. And, as in the case of big business, we can either accept the bigness with its greater efficiencies but seek to control its abuses and its extension beyond the point of increased efficiency, or we can indulge our nostalgia for the small units of the nineteenth century and atomize the existing concentration of functions. The relation between large corporations assembling end-products and subcontracting firms producing parts is not unlike the relation of big government to lesser governments. Mother-hen corporations aid their subcontractors with advice on materials procurement, accounting systems, production control, and technological advances. In the same way, big government can aid lesser governments. Pursuing the analogy further, the growth of big business in manufacturing activities where large financial resources, specialization of labor, and a national market are important factors has not meant the wholesale disappearance of small business units from activities where they can meet consumer demands as adequately as big business units. So, too, the assumption by higher governments of functions that they can perform best is not likely to lead to a denial that governments are needed at lower levels to discharge functions for whose performance the higher governments lack superior facilities.

Many intelligent observers are deeply concerned

about the growth of big business and would treat this argument by analogy as a decisive case for clipping the wings of the higher levels of government. This is not the place to probe fully into the implications of big business. It will suffice to warn that concentrations of power, whether economic or governmental, have elements of danger. The remedy, in my judgment, lies not in sacrificing the advantages to our society of large-scale organization. It lies rather in confining bigness to the fields where it produces substantial advantages for society by the more efficient and less costly production of goods and services, and in insisting upon popular controls to prevent the abuse of concentrated power.

The assurance by big government that lesser governments meet minimal standards of functional service to the people is comparable to Federal and state laws fixing minimum standards of factory safety, minimum health requirements, and minimum wages. Progressive employers may exceed the minimum. Government thereby puts a floor under the social costs of competition and free enterprise without supplanting the entrepreneur, destroying his initiative, or imposing a drab uniformity. When larger governmental areas fix floors under the social costs of lesser governmental areas' competition and self-government, there is likewise no ground for treating this as a threat to maintenance of local government with its independent status, initiative, and ability to experiment.

6

To summarize, we have noted the constitutional, political, and emotional setting of the administrative problem of governmental areas. The administrative problem proper—the reciprocal adjustment of governmental function and governmental area—was approached in the light of four factors: natural areas, administrative efficiency, fiscal adequacy, and popular control. These factors put a strain on the eighteenth and nineteenth century pattern of small local government areas and decentralized distribution of authority. At the same time that centralization has progressed to ease this strain, the smaller areas have expanded their functions, as the concept of legitimate fields of governmental activity has undergone modification. Despite the relatively greater centralization today, Cassandras who prophesy the end of local or state government ignore the areal requirements of a country as large as the United States. Such a territorial expanse requires at least three levels of governmental areas—national, subnational, and local. This being true, all three magnitudes of governmental area must meet the four tests of areal adequacy we have chosen to apply. The principal opponents of a reasonable adjustment of governmental areal arrangements are not the convinced decentralists, but the opponents of effective government, the interests whose personal status is tied to outmoded areas, and the residents of wealthy areas who are unwilling to contribute to the support of adequate services in poorer areas. By way of caution, we noted that the states, the counties, and the cities vary so much among themselves that generalizations about any category of governments need to be qualified.

We discovered two avenues to the reciprocal adjustment of governmental area and governmental function.

One was to redesign the areas themselves, either strengthening general governmental areas by establishing regional governmental areas, consolidating counties, abolishing special districts, and merging suburbs with core cities; *or* establishing separate sets of special governmental areas, each set attuned to a particular function. The other avenue was to develop more effective horizontal and vertical relations among existing governmental areas so as to mitigate the deficiencies of these areas. In the case of horizontal relations it was suggested that while large scale multi-area coöperation has educational value, it cannot approach bi- or tri-lateral coöperation as a device for getting action. But almost all horizontal coöperation among coördinate areas tends to be cumbersome and falls short of providing a fundamental adjustment of area and function.

Vertical relations, we saw, have ceased to be a matter of the mutually exclusive allocation of whole functions to one or another magnitude of governmental area. The sharing of functions, with each governmental level contributing according to its ability and intensity of interest, is the modern motif. This sharing of functions, through which the higher levels of government are increasingly making their influence felt, appears to be a means both of satisfying the citizen-customer with the quality of governmental services and of strengthening rather than weakening the lesser governmental areas.

The crucial problems to which attention needs to be directed are two. One is the devising of a strategy by which popular support can be developed for translating areal readjustment proposals into action—certainly the most appalling failure of the past generation in this field. The other is the perfecting of popular control of national, state, and local governments. While I can hardly advocate that research take a holiday, our immediate needs are not diagnosis and prescription for governmental areas. Nor, in my judgment, do we need further neat cataloguing of the advantages and disadvantages of centralization. What is needed is a means for reducing resistance to necessary areal readjustments and a revitalization of popular control in all types of governmental areas.

III: FIELD SERVICE AREAS

The basic distribution of administrative authority within each of our governments is functional. In the Federal Government only the Department of State, the Tennessee Valley Authority, and, to a lesser degree, the Department of the Interior have unique areal responsibilities. In the typical state government there are no major departments concerned with particular sections of the state, nor is there even a department of local government relations. We are so accustomed to this feature of government that it is seldom remarked. Yet area is the very foundation of legislative representation, and outweighs functional specialization in the judicial system. Only in the executive branch is the distribution of authority by function given such preëminence.[1]

Functional specialization underlies not only the primary distribution of authority among administrative departments. It also accounts for the elaborate hierarchy of bureaus, divisions, sections, and units specializing on particular activities. Almost every operating agency, however, recognizes that its job cannot wholly be performed

[1] In each of the other branches the claims of functional specialization are recognized, of course, but they are subsidiary to the main emphasis on area. Legislative bodies have functionally specialized committees. Local courts are sometimes specialized, and on collegiate courts there often develops functional specialization in the assignment of the writing of opinions.

at the capital city. An agricultural program cannot be administered without contact with farmers on their farms. Reclamation and power projects cannot be built and operated without officials at the sites. Compliance with tax laws, price controls, and labor standards cannot be checked by polite correspondence between the capital and the citizen. A field service that will span the distance from the agency headquarters to the outer bounds of the total governmental area is therefore necessary.

Once the necessity of a field service is recognized, a Pandora's box of troubles is opened. There is the problem of demarcation of field service areas and location of area headquarters. There is the problem of whether and how the field service is to be used to centralize or decentralize authority. Still more complex is the fusing of the areal organization in the field with the functional organization at the capital. All these are being wrestled with constantly by individual agencies intent primarily on effective discharge of their specialized responsibilities. Beyond such intra-agency difficulties lies the challenge to coördinate the activities of all functional agencies as they bear on each section of the country.

Guides to the demarcation of an agency's major field service areas and to its selection of headquarters cities for administration of particular functions or clusters of functions can be formulated in the light of Federal agencies' experience.[2] While I shall confine attention to the Federal problem, which is the most complex, the guides may

[2] I have drawn freely on my "Criteria for Administrative Regions," Social Forces, XXII (October 1943), 26-32. See also Legislative Reference Service, Library of Congress, Federal Field Offices (Senate Doc. No. 22, 78th Cong., 1st Sess., 1943).

be suggestive as well for state and even local governments. A first consideration is the span of control—the limitation on the number of immediate subordinates a superior official can supervise effectively. This limitation cannot be expressed as a universally valid mathematical figure. The limitation will vary with the age of the agency, the clarity of policy, the type of function, the competence of the superior, the adequacy of staff assistance for the superior, the competence of the subordinates, the objectives of the supervision, and other factors. Most Federal agencies, mindful of the span of control, have kept their principal subnational areas to less than 20. Should other considerations dictate a larger number of field service areas, these numerous, small areas must generally be placed under the wings of 20 or fewer principal field offices, each having a subnational area that includes several small areas. To facilitate our discussion, I shall use the word "region" to refer to a major subnational field service area, and the word "district" to refer to a subregional field service area.

A second consideration in establishing limits for field service areas is the nature, multiplicity, and grouping of the objects of administration—that is, of the phenomena with which the agency is concerned. It is here that one finds the greatest variety among governmental functions, for the nature, multiplicity, and grouping of tobacco farms is different from the nature, multiplicity, and grouping of banks or oil wells or meat-packing plants or Indians. This consideration draws us back to the concept of the natural area, for it is axiomatic that field service area boundaries ordinarily should not divide the natural areas, which for this purpose are the natural groupings of the objects of administration of the particular agency. Thus, agencies concerned primarily with irrigation, flood control, river navigation, and power development might be expected to establish regions corresponding to the river systems of the country, attempting so far as possible to draw areal boundaries along the ridges of watersheds. The need for avoiding division of natural areas is also apparent where agencies are dealing with Indian reservations, railroad systems, and mineral deposits. Natural commercial areas are yet another and very basic grouping of objects of administration. For agencies interested in commercial functions and for the great number of agencies whose objects of administration may be *any* citizens (as in the case of the Bureau of Internal Revenue), the area tributary to a large city from the standpoint of industry, commerce, and transportation, constitutes a natural area that should be wholly included in a field service area, either alone or with neighboring commercial areas. Commercial areas, like natural physical areas, are often no respecters of state boundaries. New York City dominates northern New Jersey and part of Connecticut more fully than it dominates northern New York. Philadelphia's commercial area includes southern New Jersey; the Chicago commercial area includes northern Indiana; St. Louis includes southern Illinois; Spokane includes northern Idaho; El Paso includes southern New Mexico; and so on.

A third consideration in laying out field service areas is the prospective workload of the field offices. Each area must be of a size to provide a workload appropriate to the most effective organization of a field office staff. Assuming a substantial but limited number of persons available for field duty, if field service areas are few in number, each area can have a large staff with a functional differentiation of duties. But, on the same assumption, if the areas are numerous, one or a few persons will have to perform all the functions of the agency in each area—functions in each of which the jack-of-all trades in a small area can scarcely have the same ability as a specialist performing exclusively a particular function for a large area. Large-scale field administration with large areas and specialized personnel is most appropriate for multi-purpose agencies. Small-scale field administration with small areas and with "generalists" predominant among field personnel is most appropriate for agencies with narrow and closely integrated types of functions.

The workload factor governs not only the number and average size of field service areas, but also the actual selection of area boundaries. Broad equalization of the workload among areas is desirable, whether the average area has a small or a large staff. If field work is so slight, appropriations so inadequate, or the number of areas so great that only one or two officials can be stationed in each area, approximate equalization of the man hours required is essential to make certain that one official is not habitually idle while a corresponding official in another area is continually overworked. At the other extreme, where the magnitude of field work necessitates a large field staff, no area should have so great a burden of work that its staff is too large for effective administration while other areas of the same agency have so little work that employment of the optimum number of functional specialists is impossible. Furthermore, regardless of the total size of the field staff, it is desirable for each field service area director to represent an equally important part of the field work if the area directors are to receive the same salary and bear the same title. Even where salary is not a consideration, the area directors are jealous of their dignity and resent the greater prestige of other area directors. This consideration, as was revealed in Work Projects Administration experience, is an important objection to the use of the 48 states as field service regions.[3]

Field service organization for a function, in the fourth place, should take account of the areas and headquarters cities already in use by governments, agencies, and private groups whose work affects that function. A specific conclusion from this consideration is that Federal agencies, such as the Public Roads Administration and the Social Security Administration, whose activities revolve about Federal grants-in-aid to the states, should ordinarily observe state lines in drawing regional boundaries. This follows naturally from the fact that much of the regional officials' time is spent in working closely with state highway commissions, state welfare departments, and similar state agencies using Federal funds. State boundaries may also be respected by Federal agencies that make extensive use of statistics either gathered by state governments or

[3] Arthur W. Macmahon, John D. Millett, and Gladys Ogden, *The Administration of Federal Work Relief* (Chicago: Public Administration Service, 1941), pp. 198-200.

compiled by other agencies that use states as their units
for compilation of data. Even when statistical information is available on county and metropolitan area bases,
the task of adding a number of these figures together to
give a total for an administrative region with irregular
boundaries is too onerous for a small regional staff.

Federal agencies coöperating with state governments
may also consider the grouping of states already in use
for purposes of interstate coöperation. The six New
England state governments have organized their interstate coöperation on a regional basis through establishment of the New England Council. Conferences of governors, highway commissioners, public health authorities,
and other state officials take place on the basis of the
New England region. Coöperation between the New
England states and Federal agencies can be advanced by
the frequent choice of New England as a Federal administrative region.

The areas already chosen by other Federal agencies
also deserve attention in the selection of boundaries for a
new set of regions. Such areas may have been tested sufficiently so that the advantages and disadvantages of the
particular areas may have been fully revealed. This is
particularly helpful where the new scheme is to serve in
the execution of a function similar to that of another
agency. Furthermore, it will be found that coöperation
among Federal agencies performing related functions is
facilitated if they are able to agree upon a common set of
regional boundaries. We shall need to return to this
problem later.

What has been said with regard to regional and district boundaries applies with perhaps even more force to the choice of regional and district headquarters cities. Where a field activity requires frequent coöperation among several agencies, that coöperation can be carried on more effectively and economically if personal and inexpensive contact can be made with the field officers of the collaborating agencies. And that clearly calls for some attention to the headquarters cities already chosen by other agencies and to the capital cities of the states.

A fifth consideration is what, for lack of a better term, may be called administrative convenience. Travel costs and travel convenience play a major role in the selection of field service area boundaries and headquarters. Occasionally an agency will even select its headquarters cities first and then use a yardstick of travel costs from each city to settle the question of area boundaries. Taking the opposite tack, with area boundaries fixed, the selection of area headquarters may well aim at placing each field staff at the point of greatest volume of work within its area. Thus, in the first World War 95 per cent of the work of the Pittsburgh Ordnance District was located within 20 miles of Pittsburgh. Although the district covered a much greater territory, the placement of headquarters at any place but Pittsburgh would have been absurd. Similarly, it is inconceivable that the headquarters of the New York Customs Comptroller's District should be any place but at New York City, even though the district includes all of New York State, Connecticut, and part of New Jersey. Curiously, the travel factor is often innocently neglected. Sometimes, for example, the upper peninsula of Michigan, all of Wisconsin, and sometimes even Minnesota and Iowa are brought into a region with Detroit as headquarters. It is discovered too late that a substantial part of the Detroit region cannot be reached by rail or highway except through Chicago, which is almost always the headquarters of another region.

There are other problems of administrative convenience than travel. In a period when construction lags behind needs, for example, the availability of office space and of satisfactory housing for field personnel enters into the selection of area headquarters cities. And where a field service area revolves about only one or two officials, rather than a large staff, the personal preferences of those officials, based on their established residences, interest in schooling for their children, and similar necessities and amenities that vary from one city to another, may play a surprisingly large role in the agency's designation of headquarters cities.

Finally, political considerations enter into the selection of boundaries and headquarters in two ways. Claims to patronage are always most insistent from political organizations and leaders whose constituencies embrace the total area within which a prospective appointee will have administrative jurisdiction. Where the 48 states are made field service areas by an agency the requirements of political clearance for area directors are most insistent, as is well illustrated by the controversy over the selection of state directors of the Office of Price Administration in 1942. If direct claims to patronage courtesies are to be avoided, field service areas should be larger than states. No political organization or person short of the

National Party Committee and the President has a *prima facie* claim to dictate the appointment of a regional director who administers an area larger than a state. Secondly, political pressure, reflecting in turn the pressures of local interests, severely handicaps the moving of field service area headquarters from one city to another or the complete discontinuance of some offices. Illustrative is the effort of the War Production Board to reduce its district offices from more than 120 to about 70. The official charged with effecting the reduction reports that "experience quickly showed that the political difficulties incident to closing some of the smaller offices were so great that it was probably worth $8,000 or $10,000 a year to keep some of these very small offices in existence, as against the tremendous loss in time and energy which must otherwise be expended by the President and Mr. Nelson [the War Production Board Chairman], as well as this organization, in dealings with Congressmen and Senators, primarily interested in maintaining the local pride of their constituents."[4] A later effort to economize by closing 23 district offices stimulated protests from 46 Senators and Representatives, not to mention chambers of commerce and individual businessmen.[5]

The field service problem of administrative geography for any single function or cluster of functions, then, is affected by six considerations: the span of control; the natural physical, social, and economic areas; the distribu-

---

[4] Quoted in Carroll K. Shaw, *Field Organization and Administration of the War Production Board and Predecessor Agencies* (Washington: Civilian Production Administration, 1947), p. 43.

[5] *Ibid.*, p. 44.

tion of workload; relations with other governments, agencies, and private groups; administrative convenience; and political factors. That these considerations do not always receive proper weight is evident enough from an examination of some Federal agencies' experience. Not infrequently an agency will slavishly and lazily follow another agency's scheme of field service areas without critical analysis of either the defects of the existing scheme for the functions it serves or the differences in functional requirements of the two agencies. Again, an agency may let one of the six relevant considerations dominate its regionalization, ignoring or weighing too lightly the other considerations. This tendency most frequently appears in an ignoring of either the natural area concept or the administrative factors.

Agencies often go astray in their efforts to discover natural physical, economic, or social areas bearing on their functional responsibilities. For example, in trying to locate the objects of administration and to equalize workload, the War Department at one time or another seriously considered gearing the boundaries of its procurement planning districts to the distribution of the male population, or to the distribution of power facilities, or to the distribution of all factories, whether large or small and whether capable or incapable of producing war goods. None of these provided a true index to the geographical distribution and productive capacities of factories for production of war goods.[6]

Finally, agencies often let accidents in the initial

---

[6] James W. Fesler, "Areas for Industrial Mobilization," *Public Administration Review*, I (Winter 1941), pp. 149-166.

stages of regionalization affect the final results. For some reason, administrative regionalists start with the magic number *twelve* as the proper number of regions. This probably dates back to the 1913 decision of Congress to create "not to exceed twelve" Federal Reserve Districts. It is, of course, necessary to start with some concept of the number of regions desired, but this number should not be such a fixed standard that violence is done to the logical grouping of objects of administration. Regional schemes also suffer on occasions from a somewhat Oriental habit of regionalizers to read from right to left. Seat them in front of a map of the United States, ask them to draw regional boundaries, and almost invariably they will start at New England and work south and west. If the regionalizer has also started with a conviction in the magic of the even dozen, he often gets to the Mississippi with only one region left. The western United States, therefore, is hustled into one region, whatever its just deserts might be. Regionalizers sometimes neglect to maintain a flexible relation between boundaries and headquarters cities. If they start with the boundary problem, headquarters selection may be slighted; if they start with headquarters cities, the boundaries may be hastily slapped on. In either event, the reciprocal relation of boundaries and headquarters will be neglected.

2

The delineation of regional and district boundaries and the selection of headquarters cities create a framework within which other problems of field service areas may be attacked. The most important of these remaining problems are two: First, the vertical distribution of authority between the national area, with headquarters at Washington, and the field service areas administered from regional and district headquarters cities; and second, the coördination within each field service area or each natural area of the several functions being performed by an agency or by several agencies in that area. The first of these problems, vertical distribution of authority, will occupy our attention for the balance of the present discussion. The second, areal coördination of functions, will be the subject of the next lecture.

There are several traps set for those who approach the question of vertical relations in a field organization. It is easy to assume that because a function is legally a Federal responsibility, the administration of the function must be highly centralized. It is almost as easy to jump to the conclusion that because an agency has established field service areas it recognizes the need for diversity in administration. Neither assumption is sound. Centralized authority for policy-making can be wedded to decentralized administration and devolution of discretionary powers. The wartime price and rationing boards of the Office of Price Administration and the local boards of the Selective Service Administration, both at the local, subdistrict level, are too recent in our memory to let the possibility of decentralized Federal administration escape us. On the other hand, the mere creation of field service areas is no guarantee of decentralization. Field organizations have their historical genesis in the need of central governments to carry their regulations and their services to citizens throughout the country. The flow may be entirely from the center to the circumference, with field agents merely executing central orders.

Another trap exists for those who wish to measure the degree of decentralization. The fact that the field service areas carry a substantial part of the workload of the agency does not necessarily mean that authority has been decentralized. A field service area may process a large number of applications from citizens. It may even give final approval or disapproval to most of them. Yet if the processing is done against detailed central instructions as to what factors shall dictate approval and what factors disapproval, the field office may be performing only a routine clerical function wholly devoid of any element of discretion.

Closely related to this snare is the assumption that there is such a thing as absolute centralization or absolute decentralization. It seems evident that what we want is a reasonable balance between centralization and decentralization. Complete centralization of a function runs up against the obvious fact of the diversities in American culture and the need for adapting administration to these diversities. Complete decentralization clashes with the need for consistency in the application of public policies and for reasonably uniform standards of equity for people wherever they may live. The task is one of statesmanship in achieving the proper balance of centralization and decentralization, not one of standing up to be counted either for centralization or for decentralization.

A further complication arises in multi-level field administration. Have we achieved decentralization when authority has been delegated by Washington to, say, three great regions headquartered at New York, Chicago, and San Francisco? Or must decentralization to be effective be pressed to the district and perhaps county and community levels? Even such a regional agency as the Tennessee Valley Authority has to face the problem of moving authority out of Knoxville to the reservoir areas. This suggests that grass roots administration may embrace too many kinds of grasses if the area involved is as large as a region. Again, I would suggest that the subtle student avoid the "either-or" dichotomy. Wartime rationing experience illustrated the need for capitalizing on all levels of a multi-level field organization, according functions to the several levels with an eye to organization of trade and industry, the intensity of local and regional pressures, and the greater specialized skills in the higher-level field offices.

To some, decentralization means much more than simple devolution of authority down the administrative hierarchy. If the grass roots are to be tapped and the spirit as well as the form of decentralization to be realized, we need to expose the field official very fully to the community of people within his jurisdictional area. Advisory committees of farmers or townspeople or leaders of particular groups may be needed. The field official himself may need to become a part of the community, sharing actively in the work of community councils, civic clubs, and similar groups. Such a concept of decentralization gets away from a narrow, sterile interpretation of the role of the administrator in modern society. At the same time, it calls for a high order of field official, one who can be a part of a community and yet not become a spokesman for local and provincial interests at the expense of the broader goals of the whole people.

3

The factors that incline an agency to move or not to move discretionary authority to its field areas are legion. As I have elsewhere attempted to isolate these in some detail,[7] I shall here simply review certain features of administrative psychology that block a vigorous policy of decentralization. Agency heads subject to being held responsible for the agency's sins of omission and commission may be reluctant to delegate authority either to heads of functional divisions at Washington or to heads of regions and districts in the field. That this violates elementary ideas of sound administration does not diminish its reality as an understandable human trait nor its significance as a bar to decentralization. The tendency, as it relates to the field service, is often nourished by functional divisions at Washington, which resist the decentralization to field service areas of important phases of their functional responsibilities, lest mistakes by field officials weaken the achievement of functional goals.

All this gets mixed up with a chicken-and-egg dilemma revolving about the competence of officials in the field service areas. The centralist tendencies I have noted are strongest in the early months and years of an agency's life, and they recur whenever policies or central organization are in a ferment. This is because a field service

---

[7] In Fritz Morstein Marx (ed.), *Elements of Public Administration* (New York: Prentice-Hall, Inc., 1946), 270-276.

cannot avoid chaos in its exercise of discretionary authority unless policy and organization at the center are reasonably clear and stable. Not unnaturally in periods of confusion or reorientation at the center, it seems important not to worse confound the confusion by turning field agents loose without guides to policy and organization. The fact that confusion is common to new agencies means that the field service is initially staffed with men content to plug away at nondiscretionary duties, to serve as "eyes and ears" of the central office, or to promote favorable public relations. By the time the agency has calmed down at the center and the question of delegation of discretionary authority to the field service areas can properly be raised, the agency may be saddled with unimaginative, nonexpert field personnel, and the central functional divisions may have developed a lack of confidence in the readiness of the field service for more substantial responsibilities. In other words, unless the agency delegates discretionary authority to the field at the start, it will not attract able men to its field staff. And if it does not attract able men at the start, it cannot subsequently delegate discretionary authority. The fact that decentralization at the start is impracticable prejudices decentralization later. In addition, by the time an agency has passed its infancy central divisions have already acquired jurisdictional prerogatives from which they resist dislodgment.

Apart from the obstacles to decentralization imposed by the early history of an agency's field service is a problem that is ever with us. This is the contrast between the specialized competence of the Washington office and the more generalized orientation of regional and district offices. The central headquarters can generally slice its functional responsibility more finely than can the field offices. Thus, a business regulatory agency can have at its headquarters separate organization units, each specializing on one of the hundreds of American industries and businesses. Too, it can have specialization by commodity or function within its legal staff. Even its administrative management units will break down such a function as personnel administration into a variety of specialties—from recreation and in-service training to classification and placement. Such specialization by groups of employees cannot be wholly reproduced at regional and district offices. A business regulatory agency clearly cannot place in each field office experts on every industry and business. Even the one or few lawyers in a field office must range up and down the whole gamut of agency activities. So too, the administrative officer has to encompass all phases of administrative management, and certainly cannot employ a specialist on each phase of personnel administration.

The Washington office, then, is a complex of specialties, while the field office is much more generalized in function and personnel. This is most evident at the district level, and perhaps clearer still in the county agent, a generalist in agriculture who contrasts sharply with the thousands of specialists in the United States Department of Agriculture's Washington office and in the state agricultural colleges.

This contrast between specialization at Washington and generalization in the field retards the process of decentralization. Specialists distrust generalists, particularly those generalists that appear at the bottom rather than the top of the organization chart and that receive lower pay than the central specialists. Distrusting field generalists' competence to handle specialized problems, the Washington specialists are reluctant to have final decision-making authority lodged in the field. In addition, the weakness of specialization in the field offices handicaps participation by field offices in the formation of agency policy. A one-man district office can usually not get its head sufficiently above the flow of operations and of paper from Washington to participate actively in national policy formation. Such an office does well if it recommends merely procedural changes and gives impressions of clientele opinion. Even at a regional office with its larger staff, the emphasis is on daily repetitive operations, and the budget often will not permit a regional director's employment of expert staff aides to contribute imagination and insight on national agency policy problems and to feed him the facts relevant to policy issues.

Using an analogy from the business world, Washington specialists regard field officials as salesmen to deliver the agency product to the customers. The skill involved is not a real specialty, developed by years of education and experience, but rather a general ability to fit into an organization and get along with the customers. The contribution a field official might make to the formation of agency policy is not dissimilar from that a salesman might make to improvement of the design of an automobile or revision of the company's plant expansion program. The reaction of Washington specialists to field officials' recommendations parallels the reaction of production engineers and skilled workmen to the salesman's suggestions.

This is, of course, a caricature, and does not accurately mirror the varying degrees of specialization in the field nor the spread between true professional specialties and off-the-cuff specialties. In addition, it does not recognize the variations among agencies in functional responsibilities. Approaching the specialists' problem with sympathy, for we cannot doubt the values in functional specialization, we can carve out some channels along which decentralization might flow. Specialization is not critically sacrificed if the agency itself has only a single function, and that a function for whose performance specific training and experience are necessary. The field agents, in such a case, can be professionally trained men whom the central specialists will respect and to whom they will be willing to decentralize authority. Similarly, even in multi-purpose agencies, the degree of sacrifice of specialization is modified if adequate funds are allotted to permit regional offices to develop specialized staffs. While such regional specialization may fall short of that at Washington, one can approach breakdowns conforming to recognized professions and skills and thus again win at least the grudging respect of Washington specialists. Pushing even this limited specialization down to the district level is almost impossible, and the district director must somehow reconcile himself to a constant flow of instructions and advice from regional and Washington offices. But decentralization to at least the regional level is often quite feasible.

A distinction may properly be drawn between the claims of true professional specialties and the claims of pseudo-professional specialties. It is clear that a medical division of a multifunctional central headquarters will not decentralize much authority to a regional or district official who has no medical training and must straddle medicine, social work, and penology in his field activities. On the other hand, there is less ground for central information officials or rationing administration officials to centralize authority exclusively on grounds of the esoteric quality of their skill and the impossibility of initiating field officials into the mystic rites of the cult.

The simple, albeit unfortunate, course chosen by many agencies is to postpone decentralization until public demand, the impossible workload of the central office, or the insistent pleas of regional and district directors force it. Thus the agency can put off resolution of the problem of adjusting less skilled field personnel to the more demanding tasks they must assume under decentralization. It can at the same time postpone a host of administrative problems. An agency administrator must spend much of his time mediating the puzzling contests between line and staff officials, between policy makers and policy executors, and among operating divisions seeking to nibble at each other's jurisdictions. To all these, which are distressing enough to an agency head, are added still other issues when an agency decentralizes. Should regional directors report to the agency head, to a staff office of field operations, or to a subordinate operating official? Do all instructions to regional directors have to clear through this central point of contact, or can functional line and staff divisions issue orders to the regional directors? Can the functional divisions communicate directly with functional specialists on the regional director's staff, or must they work through the regional directors? Can the regional office be by-passed if Washington wishes to communicate with a district office? Must important field appointments and changes of headquarters cities be cleared in advance with legislators and other political leaders of the areas involved? Should appointments of functional specialists in a region be made by the regional director or by the functional division at the center? These are all grist for vigorous debate, with the agency head as the arbiter. And they are so vital, the interests of contesting parts of the organization are so much at stake, and we are as yet so far from universally valid answers that the debate is almost continuous. Small wonder that an agency head, harassed by organizational problems of the center, may not be hospitable to decentralization with its myriad problems.

These psychological and very practical obstacles to decentralization are of course no real answer to the need for adaptation of administration to the requirements of different areas of the country. They do not outweigh the desirability of having decisions made where the relevant facts can be seen and felt rather than be processed on pieces of paper, where individual human beings and their problems—rather than only statistical aggregates—are in the range of the decision-maker's vision, where people able to contribute to sound decisions commanding public support can be consulted around a table, where the "little people" can influence agency policies as readily as the "big people's" Washington lobbyists.

4

Summarizing, we have seen that central administration, though functionally organized, must be supplemented by a field service that is areally organized. Each agency's delineation of field service areas and selection of headquarters cities can be analyzed in terms of six factors: The span of control, natural areas, workload distribution, external relations of the agency, administrative convenience, and political strategy. Common errors in arealization were noted. The balance of our discussion concerned vertical distribution of authority among the national headquarters, regions, and districts. We observed the dangers of assuming that *authority* centralized in the Federal Government must result in centralized *administration*. On the other hand, we saw that neither the mere existence of field service areas nor the fact that the field offices carry a heavy workload is a true index of decentralization. The extremes of absolute unity and anarchic decentralization were rejected for scientific purposes in favor of the quest for a sound balance between centralization and decentralization. Decentralization was seen to involve not merely Washington versus the field, but the appropriate allocation of functions among the several levels and dimensions of administrative areas—nation, regions, districts, counties, and communities. In its broader significance, decentralization was seen to go beyond mere hierarchical organization to the enrichment of field officials' experience and sympathies by full exposure to the people and their community life.   In an effort to identify some of the drags on decentralization of authority, we noted the desire of Washington officials to protect themselves against the errors of others; their conviction that crystallization of policy and organization at the center should precede decentralization to the field; their fear that specialized functions would be bungled if entrusted to field generalists rather than central specialists; and their disposition to avoid the complicated problem of gearing a strong areally organized field service to a functionally organized central office.

IV: AREAL CO-ORDINATION
OF FIELD FUNCTIONS

The most puzzling of all problems of field administration is how to fuse together the functional organization at the center with the areal organization in the field. Organization by field service areas provides a major opportunity to relate an agency's program to the needs of each particular area. While the functional principle in the central organization splits and resplits the program core until it seems not a whole but a collection of unrelated strands, the areal principle forces a braiding together of these strands before the program is brought into direct contact with the public. How to reconcile functional specialization with areal coördination is a problem that arises with regard both to the internal workings of individual agencies and to the government as a whole. We shall consider each in turn.

The internal agency problem focuses on the role of the heads of field service areas. We may call these the area generalists, for they must be concerned with all phases of the agency's program, as contrasted with the specialists on particular functions that contribute to that program. Before we direct our thinking to the role of the area generalist, however, it is important to look first at the central organization.

Let me advance the thesis that field problems are less *sui generis* than a mirroring of problems at the center. If the thesis is sound, the ignoring of it can lead us into extravagant demands and impossible organizational arrangements for field service areas. An immediate conclusion from the thesis is that the strength of the area generalist is dependent upon the strength of the generalist at the center.

Unfortunately, the generalist at the center is often in a weak position. The head of almost any major agency of the Federal Government is far less the issuer of orders down a firm chain of command, which the layman and the less sophisticated student of organization charts assume, than he is an uneasy presider over a loose confederation of autonomous and semi-autonomous bureaus. The agency head is often a bird of flight. He enters his post needing months and even years of education in the activities of the agency. He may leave before he has completed that education or before he has more than started a long-range program designed to change the policies and organization of the agency. Bureau chiefs, on the other hand, may be permanent officials, possibly wedded to the ways they have been doing things and certainly indisposed to bend to the vagaries of each new occupant of the agency head's office. Each bureau has its own long-range program, often imperfectly articulated with the programs of other bureaus in the agency. If politically astute, each bureau has its own contacts with legislators and legislative committees, and has geared its distinctive clientele to pressure group defense of bureau autonomy.

To see what this means for the field, assume that an

agency head inquires into his agency's field organization. He will generally find that each bureau has its own field service, each operating through a distinctive pattern of field service areas, each choosing cities and office buildings for field headquarters without regard to the choices made by other bureaus in the department. There is in no area a spokesman to the public for the agency as a whole. Each field official speaks only for his bureau. Field officials operating in the same general area for different bureaus have never met each other, let alone coöperated on inter-bureau matters. There has been no study of what the impact of the agency's total program on an area is, nor of what it should be. There is no one in the area to act for the agency head in coördinating agency policies, line operations, or housekeeping services. There is no agency policy on decentralization of authority, each bureau making its own choice regardless of the implications for the agency and for the government as a whole.

Here is an open field in which the agency head might assert his authority, improve agency operations, and bring government closer to the people. Yet what usually happens? In many an agency the bureaus so firmly resist reform that no real change is effected. Taking a leaf from the filibusterer's book, they capitalize on dilatory tactics. They know that in time the Administration will change and a new agency head will have to start from scratch. In other agencies a sop is tossed the agency head in the form of a specious but protean uniformity of field service areas, with some departures from common boundaries for functional reasons, and with many departures from the ideal of common headquarters cities. A strong agency head may win the right to appoint area generalists—regional and district directors for the agency as a whole. But the bureaus then balk at the vesting of any authority in such area generalists. The area generalist may make speeches to civic organizations in the area to publicize the department. He may direct such house-keeping services as office space, supplies, travel, and financial accounting. He may even assemble the specialists' weekly reports and write a covering memorandum so that at least formally there is a regular agency-wide report from the area to the agency head. Lucky the agency head who achieves even this much before his term of office expires and the bureaus quickly backslide from their enforced state of grace. To try to press beyond this point with the generalist approach to field service areas may mean for the agency head on the one side and the bureau directors on the other to take up prepared positions and settle down to an indecisive thirty years' war.

All that I am trying to suggest is that those who clamor for areal coördination of an agency's functions, however laudable their motives, should first wrestle with the problem of agency integration at the center. For unless the agency head at the center can truly unify his confederation of bureaus and so underpin the role of generalists throughout the agency, it is futile to expect his counterpart in the field, the area generalist, to exhibit signs of strength.

Before leaving this problem of central organization, it should be made clear that the argument assumes neither a pusillanimous agency head nor a set of bureau chiefs intent upon undermining sound organization or serving special interests. An able, strong agency head may quite reasonably conclude that the strength of his agency lies in the strength of its bureaus; that in the Federal government the agency heads are simply intermediate layers between the bureaus that "do the work" and the President who, if his span of control permitted, might better be put in direct contact with bureau chiefs; that the bureaus huddled under the same agency tent really have little in common despite the reshuffling of bureaus among departments by administrative reorganizers; and that in fact individual bureaus may need coördination in the field with bureaus located in other agencies more than they need coördination with bureaus under the common tent. By the same token, it should be clear that bureaus that defend their autonomy may start from this same theory of administrative organization—a theory that can literally be called "bureaucracy," government by bureaus, in contrast to "departmentocracy," government by departments. With this philosophy are linked further bureau viewpoints. There is among able administrators the conviction that the function of one's own bureau is far more important to the public interest than such "outsiders" as agency heads can be expected to appreciate. Consequently, the public is better served if the function is kept within the control of the bureau itself, rather than exposed to the whims of a generalist. The emphasis in the Federal government on functional responsibility means that each bureau chief lives in fear of being pilloried for failure to achieve functional goals important to the people as a whole or to particular interest groups. His natural impulse is to keep all activities associated with his function, whether central or field, under his direct control. He does not dare, if given a choice, expose his function to possible bungling by central or area generalists outside his own control.

2

Even if the agency head and his bureau chiefs have somehow arrived at a master set of field service areas for the agency, with common headquarters cities, and if the area generalist is expected to be more than a speech-maker and office boy, important questions of administrative relationship remain. These questions all relate to whether and how the spectrum of agency functions can be concentrated into a beam for transmission to a field service area, there perhaps to be dispersed again into the constituent functions. An initial setting for any solution is the fact that the headquarters of each major field service area is usually functionally organized in a generally parallel fashion to that at Washington. There will be an area generalist paralleling the agency head, and each section of his staff will parallel a major bureau at Washington. In this setting there are two major answers to the basic question. One is to assume that the agency head at Washington so well coördinates policies among his bureaus that there are no major conflicts, to let each bureau appoint personnel in and issue orders to its corresponding sections in the field service areas, to have the area generalist encourage practical adjustments among the sections in the area largely on the basis of his prestige and personality and the recognition by the sections of the need for harmonious working relations, and to let the area generalist report to Washington any inter-section difficulties that cannot be resolved by agreement at his level. This is the functional approach, involving strong and direct functional lines of authority between bureaus at Washington and their microcosms in the field service areas, and leaving the area generalist as one who simply contributes his good offices as a mediator among sections. The second major answer is to require that all bureaus at Washington submit proposed field orders to the agency head or his deputy, who may review and revise such orders and who is the sole channel for transmission of orders to the field; to have such orders go directly to the area generalist, who delivers them to his section heads with any supplementary instructions he finds necessary; and to expect the area generalist to have genuine responsibility for performance of all agency functions in the area. This is the area approach, involving strong and direct generalist lines of authority between the agency head or his deputy at Washington and the generalist in the field service area. It leaves the functional bureaus at Washington in the role of staff advisers of the agency head on agency policy and field administration, and makes the functional sections in field service areas the subordinates of the area generalist.

It is not difficult to see why the generalist is dissatisfied with the first approach and the functionalist dissatisfied with the second. As a result, agencies go through a succession of compromises designed to leave both parties equally unhappy, which supposedly leads to greater harmony. The forms that compromise may take are various. I direct your attention to the experience of the Department of State, the Government's office of field operations for foreign areas, as recorded by Arthur W. Macmahon and Leonard D. White; of the Federal relief agencies, as jointly recorded by Macmahon, John D. Millett, and Gladys Ogden; of the War Production Board, as recorded by Carroll K. Shaw; of the Office of Price Administration, as recorded by Emmette S. Redford; of the Department of Agriculture, as recorded by David B. Truman; of the Public Works Administration, as recorded by J. Kerwin Williams, and of the industrial mobilization planning units of the War Department, which I have elsewhere attempted to summarize.[1] The experiences of these agencies reveal that no compromise between the functionalists and the area generalists amounts to much more than a precarious balance of power, that the agency head must swing his influence back and forth much as Great Britain has historically done in relation to the European powers, and that the plaudits for the agency head will be those appropriate to an enforcer of an armed truce rather than those accorded a real peacemaker.

[1] Arthur W. Macmahon, "Function and Area in the Administration of International Affairs," in Leonard D. White, *et al., New Horizons in Public Administration* (University, Ala.: University of Alabama Press, 1945), pp. 119-143; Leonard D. White, "Field Coördination in Liberated Areas," *Public Administration Review,* III (Summer 1943), 187-193; Arthur W. Macmahon, John D. Millett, and Gladys Ogden, *The Administration of Federal Work Relief* (Chicago: Public Administration Service, 1941); Carroll K. Shaw, *Field Organization and Administration of the War Production Board and Predecessor Agencies* (Washington: Civilian Production Administration, 1947); Emmette S. Redford, *Field Administration of Wartime Rationing* (Washington: U. S. Government Printing Office, 1947); David B. Truman, *Administrative Decentralization* (Chicago: University of Chicago Press, 1940); J. Kerwin Williams, *Grants-in-Aid under the Public Works Administration* (New York: Columbia University Press, 1939); James W. Fesler, "Areas for Industrial Mobilization," *Public Administration Review,* I (Winter 1941), 149-166. Subsequent references to OPA experience are based on Redford's able study.

An important effort to give theoretical underpinning to one type of compromise is represented by Macmahon's and Millett's formulation of the theory of dual supervision. Millett ably defended the theory in a 1944 lecture in this same series at the University of Alabama.[2] The theory of dual supervision throws overboard the Biblical injunction that man cannot serve two masters, substituting therefor a belief that the functional man in a field service area can have a dual allegiance—one to his functional counterpart at Washington and one to the area generalist. The tolerableness of such dual allegiance depends on the mutual forbearance and understanding of the generalist and the specialist. The area generalist "must recognize the limitations of his own technical capacity, must appreciate that his role essentially is coördinative and facilitative, must seek the best means of realizing the objectives of the technician within the limitations of a common organization. He sees general objectives and general obstacles; he is the recipient of orders from above on major strategy and must use his discretion in adapting those orders to the local situation." On the other hand, "the subject-matter specialist is the functional expert, his the knowledge of detail that must ultimately mean success or failure. But both his professional and in-service training need to give him a sense of organizational patterns and procedures, or orderly relationships, so that he may comprehend the needs and purpose of the whole enterprise."[3]

2 John D. Millett, "Field Organization and Staff Supervision," in White, et al., op. cit., pp. 96-118.

3 Macmahon, Millett, and Ogden, op. cit., p. 268.

I am not sure that segregating the area supervisor from the functional supervisor by giving them separate but equal accommodations will dull the query, "In a pinch, which gets the *superior* accommodations?" It is true, of course, that an area generalist, like every generalist, must recognize his own limitations and in ordinary cases must not overrule the technical advice and actions of his accountant, medical officer, personnel officer, or economist. It is also true that the functional specialists in field service areas will do a better job if their corresponding functional specialists at Washington advise them of the best technical practices as revealed by experience in other field service areas or by discoveries of the research staff at Washington. This seems to me no more questionable than for functional specialists in field service areas to subscribe to professional journals and attend professional meetings in order to improve their technical competence. It is quite a different thing though to say that functional specialists in the areas must take *orders* from their counterparts in Washington on matters related to the specialty, with the area generalist having no significant discretion on such matters. The area generalist, as Millett has defined him, has principally the job of getting the greatest efficiency with the greatest economy. His role is described as threefold: To direct the central house-keeping services; to be the principal contact man or public relations man; and to work out desirable solutions of common interests among the specialties, presumably as a mere mediator, and so maintain "harmony at all times between the parts."[4]

---

[4] Millett, *op. cit.*, p. 115.

This is, in my judgment, to return to a minimal concept of the area generalist's role. I venture the suggestion that the experience of the Office of Price Administration and the War Production Board reveals that coincident with the arrival of each agency at maturity came a strengthening of the area generalist. In September 1943, for example, after unhappy experience under a strict dual supervision formula, OPA issued an order under which "the regional administrators and district directors were given full authority for direction of all OPA operations in areas subject to their jurisdiction." In the War Production Board, the passage of time saw strengthening of the authority of regional directors in the making of appointments, the organizing of their regional office staffs, and the preparation and execution of budgets for their offices. In parallel fashion, the functional divisions at Washington suffered a curtailment of authority to issue general instructions to field offices.

My doubts about the universal value of the dual supervision doctrine stem in part from strategic considerations. Our major task is twofold: To fashion some unity and coherence from the multiple specialties at Washington so that for any field service area there is a consistent agency program involving the least possible waste motion and embarrassment from conflicting activities, and to establish a framework through which decentralization of authority can take place so that in each field service area the agency's operations can be adapted to distinctive local needs. Both phases of the task require an uphill struggle. Functional divisions at Washington are not going to yield up autonomous control of their field activities unless faced by a strong emphasis on control by generalists at national and area levels. And decentralization will not be firmly embraced by Washington divisions in the absence of pressure by a corps of generalists who lack some of the perfectionism of technicians and are aware of the significance of decentralization for the future of American government. In other words, functionalists typically resist both integration of agency programs on an areal basis and decentralization to field officials.[5] Because neither issue is ever settled once and for all, we shall need generalists to hold the fort, once it is won, against the resurgence of the functional autonomists. How often must we be reminded that experts should be on tap and not on top?

Actually, we cannot arrive at a single formula to cover all agencies. An old-line executive department, with a long tradition of bureau autonomy and with a congeries of only slightly related functions, is in a less favorable position to press toward departmental field service areas under strong generalists than is a new agency with no traditions to buck, with fluidity in its organization structure, and with all its functions centering about a common objective. Between these two extremes lies a variety of situations. For example, the Office of Price Adminis-

---

[5] In the preceding chapter I have indicated that functional specialists will more readily decentralize to specialists in the field than to area generalists. This remains true within the narrow bounds of the specialty. But they will rarely decentralize to facilitate inter-specialty integration and adaptation of the specialty to the larger concerns of the people in an area. That is, they hesitate to authorize field specialists to participate in joint programming and coördinated operations in the area independently of specific Washington approval of every commitment by the field generalists.

tration, though a new agency with a vigorous executive, had difficulty in arriving at a regime of strong area generalists, partly because it embraced three distinct programs—price control, rent control, and rationing—each of which was entrusted to a distinct "department" within the agency. OPA also made initial errors by inept choice of area generalists and by recognition of strong functional lines of authority between specialists in Washington and specialists in the field service areas, which prejudiced its later efforts to strengthen the area generalists. Similarly, the War Production Board, though a new agency, never realized as strong a role for the area generalists as might have been possible if its predecessor agencies had willed it a single field service instead of several separate field organizations, or if WPB top officials had been as interested in coördinating field operations as they were in coördinating policy formation.

The diversity of functions, organization, and maturity among Federal agencies means that we cannot jump swiftly to a few master sets of field service areas, one for each major agency, or to a uniform resolution of the conflict of powers between area generalists and functional specialists. Progress should be most rapid with individual bureaus rather than with large departments, and with agencies having a common core of purpose rather than with multi-purpose agencies, such as the Federal Security Agency, that are relatively new "holding companies" for previously independent agencies.[6]

---

[6] A perceptive examination of the Federal Security Agency's field coördination problem was made in Office of Administration, Federal Security Agency, *Methods and Approaches for Improving Field Coördination within*

3

These observations on intra-bureau and intra-departmental coördination of field functions suggest how far we are from any adequate response to the need for government-wide inter-agency coördination of functions on an areal basis. The Federal government has at least a generation of experience with field coördination of Federal agencies, ranging from the Bureau of the Budget's regionalized Federal Coördinating Service and local Federal Business Associations prominent in the 1920's, through the National Emergency Council's State Directors in the 1930's, to the present field offices of the Bureau of the Budget.[7] In addition, during the war years, important experience was accumulated in the field coördination of selected agencies interested in common problems, particularly through the Committee for Congested Production Areas, the Office of Defense Health

the *Federal Security Agency* (multilithed, May 20, 1947), a report prepared by Dean Snyder, Elton Woolpert, and Harry Holland. In July 1948, acting in accordance with the Agency's 1949 Appropriation Act, the Federal Security Administrator established Agency regional offices and initiated action to bring the regional areas and offices of constituent units of the Agency into conformity with the master plan. Each regional director was given "general administrative supervision over the principal representatives of constituent organizations who are stationed in or detailed to the Region." It will take a strong Administrator indeed to convert this brave statement into reality. See Federal Security Agency Press Release 385, July 9, 1948, and Federal Security Agency Orders 16, 16-1, and 16-2, July 30, 1948.

[7] This experience, up to 1936, is summarized in my "Executive Management and the Federal Field Service," in U. S. President's Committee on Administrative Management, *Report with Special Studies* (Washington: U. S. Government Printing Office, 1937), pp. 271-294.

and Welfare Services, and the joint work of the War Production Board and War Manpower Commission.[8]

This experience has had enough common features to warrant certain generalizations about inter-agency coördination. The diversity of field service area patterns has left field officials of different agencies without a common geographical basis of coöperation. Even if all regional officials in a given city such as Atlanta are sympathetic to coöperation, it is quickly discovered that the regional official of agency "A" can speak only for a three-state area, the official of agency "B" wants coöperation covering his ten-state area, and the other officials fall in between, some even being concerned with natural areas centering in Atlanta that have no relation to state boundaries. The diversity of area headquarters cities also limits the ease of coöperation. Even if several agencies recognize a common Southern field service area, the fact that Richmond, Atlanta, Birmingham, and New Orleans may be the respective headquarters for the agencies reduces the facility with which their regional directors can, literally and figuratively, get together. To press the same point further, the failure of the Federal government to house agency field staffs in the same buildings at common headquarters cities impedes coöperation, particularly coöpera-

---

8 This experience is reviewed in Corrington Gill, "Federal-State-City Coöperation in Congested Production Areas," *Public Administration Review*, V (Winter 1945), 28-33; Alvin Roseman, "The Regional Coördination of Defense Health and Welfare Services," *Public Administration Review*, I (Autumn 1941), 432-440; Office of Community Services, Federal Security Agency, *Teamwork in Community Services, 1941-1946* (Washington: Federal Security Agency, 1946); and Shaw, *op. cit.*

tion of the informal two-agency type. To the layman this may seem not an important handicap. The testimony of Federal officials contradicts the lay judgment. In many a city it is even impossible to get the field staffs of bureaus of the same executive department common housing, which handicaps the efforts of the department head to set up common regional housekeeping services on accounting, budgeting, travel, office supplies, and personnel, as well as his efforts to develop department consciousness among the field staffs.

The soil for inter-agency coördination must be prepared by promotion of familiarity by each agency with related agencies' program and operations and by promotion of personal acquaintanceship and informality among officials of related agencies. Again I feel that this consideration would be ranked quite differently by laymen and by those who have really grappled with inter-agency coördination problems in the field. Coördination, as a triangular approach calling for harmonizing of the activities of two officials by a mediating third party, must be complemented by two-way coöperation that in many negotiations makes a third party superfluous. And two-way coöperation can flourish only among officials who are familiar with one another's activities and problems and can deal with one another on a personal and informal basis, instead of as embodiments of the majesty of their respective agencies. Put in different words, I am saying that two-way coöperation (and, by implication, triangular coördination) is conditioned by that central problem of public administration—effective communication.

Coördination among agencies needs to be nurtured

by some neutral agency that is a staff arm of the President. This is true of coördination at Washington. It is also true of coördination in the field. As I conceive a field coördinator concerned with the whole range of governmental activities, he would be a mediator, a conciliator, or, in Arnold Brecht's phrase, a "regional convener." He would not be "a little President"; he would not have authority to make decisions that would bind the agencies operating in his area. This, you will note, contrasts with my disposition to give real authority to the area generalists of executive agencies having a central core of common functions. It is a contrast but not, in my judgment, an inconsistency. A departmental area generalist might become familiar enough with the department's total activities to have the informational basis for sound decisions, while the governmental regional coördinator could not sufficiently master the tremendous range of governmental activities to be trusted with decisive authority. Areal coördination of functions within a department does not destroy the functional responsibility principle of the executive branch, for area generalists' decisions would be challengeable before the department head by the Washington functional bureaus. But vesting decision-making powers in a governmental regional coördinator would sever functional lines even of the executive departments and leave no point of reconciliation of function-area conflicts short of the President himself.

Inter-agency coördination of field activities, like so many phases of field administration, requires coördination at the center even more than it requires on-the-spot coördination in field service areas. Most of the major field conflicts—that between the Work Projects Administration and the Public Works Administration, that between the War Production Board and the Army Service Forces, or that between the Bureau of Reclamation and the Army Corps of Engineers—have stemmed from poor coördination at Washington, a failure to define agency functions clearly, or a failure to resolve differences in concepts of the public interest. Problems of this character cannot be satisfactorily resolved at a dozen different regional centers. All that the field can contribute, and it is a significant service, is the early reporting of evidences of conflict and overlapping so that a vigorous President, aided by the Bureau of the Budget, can make prompt adjustments at Washington to prevent development of a nationwide vendetta between agencies. This reporting of field evidences of conflict can be a continuous responsibility of the governmental regional coördinator. It should not, though, be solely of an *ad hoc* character. An orderly comprehensive study of the total impact of Federal functions on a sample area offers an opportunity for orienting Washington on the needs for fundamental reappraisal of agencies' jurisdictions and performance. The sample area need not be as large as a region; it might be only a county or city. Because the impact of Federal activities is different in the South from that in, say, the Pacific Northwest, studies of this character should be conducted in each of the major regions of the country.

Since mid-1943 the burden of inter-agency field coördination on a government-wide basis has been carried by the Bureau of the Budget. For a description of this activity we must rely on a study prepared by Earl Latham in late 1944, when most of the Bureau's field offices were less than a year old.[9] It is to be hoped that some student of public administration will undertake a more nearly current analysis of this significant experiment.

By the end of 1944, the Bureau of the Budget had four field offices, located in Dallas, Chicago, Denver, and San Francisco. They were established to "secure for the Bureau information concerning the operations of the Federal Government in the field, promote economical and efficient administration in field establishments of Federal agencies, and lend such assistance in the field as may be requested by the divisions" of the Bureau.[10] Latham has noted four specific duties flowing from this general mission: (1) "to counsel and advise with federal officials in the field for the purpose of getting better coördination of federal programs and better relations among the federal agencies in the field;" (2) "to consult with officials of state and local governments on the operation of federal programs of concern to them and to report to bureau headquarters problems arising in these relationships, with recommendations for their solution;" (3) "to examine and recommend improvements in the utilization of supplies and equipment in the field;" and (4) "to make administrative studies on the initiation of the field offices or, at the request of other bureau staff, to make recommendations for more efficient operations

9 Earl Latham, "Executive Management and the Federal Field Service." *Public Administration Review,* V (Winter 1945), 16-27.

10Quoted in *ibid.,* p. 19, from Bureau of the Budget Office Memorandum No. 100, July 24, 1943.

and to report to bureau headquarters those problems requiring special study or action or a policy statement or guide from headquarters."[11] Of these functions, the fourth has been dominant, and here the initiative for the making of administrative studies has come in most cases from the Bureau staff in Washington. In the other three functions—inter-agency coördination, consultation with state and local officials, and improvement in utilization of supplies and equipment—the principal emphasis appears to have been on housekeeping activities, procedural coördination of fact-gathering surveys, and guiding of inquirers to appropriate operating agencies. These are all important services. But they fall short of getting interfunctional coöperation at the program and planning rather than the procedural level, to the end that the combined impact of Federal programs on a given region will be consistent with the needs of the people of that region.

It may be that the Bureau has felt the need to move cautiously at first in order to win the confidence of operating agency officials both at Washington and in the field. It may be that, as a staff agency that stresses its non-operating character, the Bureau has discovered that its field offices are orphans in their regions. They are to provide staff assistance, but to whom? There is no "little President" in the region to receive the advice and to move with prestige into a situation where field agents of several departments cannot be cajoled into agreement by the gentle counsel of a staff-type office, and so need mediation of a higher level. In contrast, the Washington office

[11]Latham, *op. cit.*, p. 19.

of the Bureau, while staff in character, can resort directly to the President for top-level mediation and even decisive coördinative action. There is some danger, therefore, that the Bureau field offices will confine their activity to the conducting of special field studies for the Bureau's Washington office and the facilitation of procedural coöperation among agencies in the field. Let me repeat that this is needed activity, even if it does not capture the full promise of areal coördination of the functions of the Federal government.

4

We have attempted to probe the problem of areal coördination of the field functions of a central government. A major conclusion is that both in analysis and in prescription as much attention must be paid to the administrative organization at the center as is paid to administrative arrangements in the field. Confusion at the center will be reflected in confusion in the field. The relative strength of generalists and functionalists at the center will fix the strength of their counterparts in the field. The simplicity or complexity of the agency's or the government's functions and the identity or diversity of clienteles served will affect the ease of areal coördination.

Another conclusion is that the conflict between the areal and the functional bases of organization is never wholly resolved. The functional basis is historically in the stronger position, and any advance toward real areal coördination requires affirmative efforts by the generalists at the center. The result is often a compromise, but generally one in which either function or area is accepted as the dominant line of authority and responsibility, and the other is accepted as a channel for advice and counsel. The doctrine of "dual supervision," which in theory denies the need for one or the other to be dominant, actually tends to rationalize one form of compromise—that of functional dominance (though that apparently was not the intent of the doctrine's proponents)—in terms that may confuse thousands of functional field officials by making each the judge of which of two masters he shall obey in case of conflicting instructions.

Progress would seem to lie instead along two lines: the strengthening of the area generalist in each agency that has a closely related bundle of functions and whose Washington organization is more than a confederation of bureaus; and the confining of the area generalist to a merely mediating role where he is concerned with all the functions of a government or with a congeries of only slightly related functions belonging to a poorly integrated department.

V: EMERGING AREAL PATTERNS OF INTERGOVERNMENTAL AND INTERAGENCY CO-OPERATION

Imagination and inventiveness are needed if we are ever to bring to a focus in each area the multiplicity of governmental functions affecting the people of the area. A number of experiments are currently in progress. Among the most significant are the valley authority, the Department of the Interior's areal coördination work in the Pacific Northwest and the Missouri Basin, the Pacific Coast Board of Intergovernmental Relations, and the county councils on intergovernmental relations.

Resource development is the core of the most dramatic and challenging assertion of the primacy of area over function. It is institutionally embodied in the valley authority, responsible to no functional department at Washington, and charged with direct responsibility for multiple-purpose planning and development of the water resources of a drainage basin. The Tennessee Valley Authority has come to symbolize the potentialities of decentralization and areal coördination. Its remarkable record of achievement of higher living standards and economic well-being for the people of the Tennessee Valley, its effective coördination of its functional units, and the weaving into its whole fabric of the strand of grass roots coöperation with state and local governments have won for TVA the plaudits of students the world over. Success invites imitation, and a Missouri Valley Authority, a Columbia Valley Authority, and other like agencies have been strongly advocated. Objective appraisal of such proposals in terms of our interest in the reciprocal adjustment of function and area is difficult, in large part because the debates over such proposals have been shot through with conflict between public power and private power interests, with not always judicious use of the symbolism of "centralized bureaucracy" and "grass roots democracy," and with uncritical assumption of the ready transferability of the TVA experience to other regions.

The appeal of the valley authority idea stems not only from the notable success of TVA, but as well from the historically well-founded doubt that functional bureaus and departments of the Federal Government can coördinate their activities on either a national or an areal basis. There is here a neat reversal of the proposition that the incompetence of local government in performing even local area functions justifies much of the transference of power to higher levels of government. Now it is argued that incompetent coördination of functions at Washington forces devolution of powers to quasi-autonomous regional authorities. While it would be impossible to ignore the intimate relation between water resources functions and drainage basin areas as foci for coördination, I wish to emphasize that in a sense the basic problem is national, rather than areal. Such related units as the Corps of Engineers and the Bureau of Reclamation, both concerned with water resources, are in separate departments at Washington. So too are the Forest Service and the National Park Service, both concerned in substantial measure with the use of forested public lands. Being in distinct departments, such units have no coördinating superior short of the overburdened President. Their only real coördination is through formal interdepartmental negotiation, and even that often requires a good shove from Congress, as in the merging of the Pick and Sloan plans for development and control of the waters of the Missouri.

The difficulty is often misjudged as solely one of bureaucratic jealousies and fear of consolidation of staffs with loss of positions for some employees. This is an important phase of the problem. But even more significant is a long history of different concepts of the public interest, different interest group clienteles, different sources of political support, responsibility to Congress through different committees, and ancient prejudices against Cabinet members long passed from the scene. The Corps of Engineers of the War Department, technically competent, proud of a long tradition of quasi-autonomy, and commanding effective political support, emphasizes flood control and navigation as the principal phases of water resources. The Bureau of Reclamation of the Interior Department, like the Engineer Corps staffed with competent engineers and engaged in the building of dams, and in its own right politically strong in the western states, emphasizes the use of water for irrigation and reclamation of arid land. Into this traditional duality of interest are now interjected such emphases as control of floods downstream (where the Corps of Engineers has been most active) by the damming of "little waters" upstream (where the Bureau of Reclamation has been active); the use of publicly built dams for public generation of power, which requires a different design of dams and brings the Federal Power Commission into the picture; the absorption of water in the soil and the prevention of silting of rivers and reservoirs through forestation and soil conservation work of the Department of Agriculture; the prevention of pollution of public water supplies, a concern of the U. S. Public Health Service in the Federal Security Agency; and the protection of fish through the Interior Department's Fish and Wildlife Service.

I have emphasized complexity, because that is the problem. Despair over unraveling the tangled skein at Washington accounts for the eager welcome for the proposal of a valley development authority that will supplant the Corps of Engineers and Bureau of Reclamation as dam-constructing agencies for the valley, and either supplant other water resource and related land resource agencies or set the terms for their entry into the valley. Thus the Gordian knot is deftly cut, and areal coördination of Federal water resource functions is assured.

The valley authority, therefore, provides one of the major instruments for the reciprocal adjustment of function and area. It is illusory, however, to think that it brings no problems of its own or that it solves all those to which we have been directing our attention. Note first that not all governmental functions are expected to be performed in a valley area by the valley authority. Not only do most state and local powers remain unimpaired, but Federal functions unrelated to water resources continue to be administered through the field agents of Washington-based bureaus. Collection of taxes; prosecution of violations of Federal laws; delivery of the mail; recruitment of soldiers, sailors, and aviators; most lending activities; census-taking; regulation of rail, air, and highway transportation; radio regulation; and many other Federal responsibilities would be functionally administered by regular Federal departments and commissions. The valley authority, then, does not pretend to be an instrument for coördination of all Federal administrative functions on an areal basis, nor obviously is its role that of a comprehensive coördinator of horizontal and vertical relations among Federal, state, and local governments active in the area.

The valley authority, as presently conceived and as exemplified in TVA, is a wholly Federal agency that is hierarchically responsible to a nationally elected President and a national Congress. It is not a joint creature of Federal, state, and local governments of the area, nor is it responsible, in the literal sense of democratic government, to the people of the valley in which it operates. In legal status it is as much a part of the Federal Bureaucracy as the Department of the Interior or the Treasury Department. A majority of its directing board, as in the case of TVA, may be from outside the region, and its key staff members may also be recruited nationally. Accurate analysis of the valley authority, therefore, cannot be based on a glowing conviction that here is the epitome of grass roots democracy. The misapprehension on this point is due to the fact that, despite TVA's legal powers and relationships, the directors and staff of TVA have recognized the practical necessity of winning local support and have recoiled from a paternalistic role that might poison the well-springs of state and local governments. As a result, TVA has deliberately built up a network of contractual grant-in-aid agreements with state and local governments in the area, farming out to them tasks that TVA might have done more speedily and at times more competently, but not without sapping some vitality from the valley's own governments.

In terms of our earlier explorations, the valley authority as represented by TVA is a device for meeting the Federal government's problem of field service areas. It assures uniform area boundaries and common headquarters cities for Federal water-resource functions. It provides for decentralization of Federal administrative authority over water resources to a particular field service area. It resolves the competitive pulls of functional and areal lines of responsibility by decisively clipping the functional lines leading to Washington water-resource agencies, substituting therefor an area-based valley authority co-equal in status with the great function-based executive departments. Though its offices be in such a city as Knoxville, it remains a Congressional creation responsible for its stewardship to the whole people, and not, in any direct way, to the people of its valley.

The multiplication of valley authorities will create new puzzles for students of public administration. We have earlier observed that function has been the basic principle of executive branch organization in the Federal government, and that the idea of areal coördination has developed late and as a secondary principle supplementing, but not generally supplanting, the functional lines of authority. Suppose now that the country is blanketed with valley authorities, each with a monopoly of power over Federal water-resource functions in its valley. Immediately our problem is reversed. Now area dominates the line of authority and several difficulties emerge. One is whether the Washington water-resource agencies are to be reduced from operating organizations to staff units furnishing only advice and occasionally detailing personnel to the valley authorities if the latter choose to invite such aid in preference to building their own technical staffs. Another difficulty is the need to have some kind of national coördination for each function if Congress and the President are to continue to have distinguishable and internally consistent national policies on power, navigation, reclamation, soil conservation, recreation, and like subjects. Perhaps most important, there must be some machinery for making the total program of each valley authority consistent with the total programs of the other valley authorities. At first glance it may appear that each valley's water program is so distinct that there can be no conflicts and duplications such as have plagued national functional agencies. But consider how what is done on the Tennessee or the Missouri affects flood levels on the lower Mississippi, how TVA's marketing of its electricity ranges far beyond the bounds of the Tennessee Valley, how the Pacific Northwest's development of a phosphate fertilizer industry may need to be related to TVA's nationally marketed fertilizer, and how the public may need education on why a TVA is withdrawing submarginal lands from cultivation while a Missouri Valley Authority is bringing arid lands into cultivation by irrigation. Finally, the government must build a bridge between the area-based water-resource authorities and the function-based bureaus carrying on activities tangential to the valley authorities' work. As an example, what the Securities and Exchange Commission does about utility holding company structures or the Interstate Commerce Commission does about rail-water and interterritorial freight rates may bear directly on valley authorities' interests. How in such cases will function and area be reciprocally adjusted?

The valley authority idea starts a chain of speculations both about how this new idea is to be absorbed in our governmental structure and about the availability of alternatives. Should most water-resource functions of the Federal government be assigned to the Department of the Interior or, perhaps, a new department? If this were done, could the Department, with its current trend toward decentralization and areal coördination of its bureaus, provide a tolerable substitute for semi-autonomous valley authorities? If not, should all valley authorities be made responsible to the Secretary of the Interior or a new Cabinet-level official, rather than directly to the President and Congress? As a separate line of speculation, should the Department of the Interior be confined principally to functions relating to the western part of the United States, where public lands focus much of its attention already? If so, would there be material gains in moving the headquarters of the national Department of the Interior to a western city like Denver, on the analogy of the Tennessee Valley Authority's making Knoxville rather than Washington its principal office? If the Department of the Interior were thus made a Department of the West, might it be made responsible for development of such western valleys as the Missouri, Columbia, and Colorado? Should such development be based on separate valley authorities or on the concept that the Department is itself a great regional authority which, like TVA, might act both through functional units and through area management offices?

The proposal of a Missouri Valley Authority is resisted by many residents of the Missouri Valley because of fear that such a purely Federal authority would reduce the vitality of state and local governments. Is there any way that a valley authority can be made an effective instrument of intergovernmental collaboration and coördination—thus going far beyond the areal coördination of Federal government functions? This objective cannot be fully achieved by the authority's gracious inviting of advice from state and local officials or by the use of state and local agencies as agents of the authority under grant-in-aid arrangements. We need penetrating thought on how a joint Federal-state-local authority might be created without substantial impairment of the Federal government's constitutional responsibilities and without blinking the fact that the heaviest expenditures would be out of funds contributed by the people of the whole nation.

These and like questions are suggestive of the wide range of problems to which students of administration need to address themselves if the valley authority is to be fitted into our governmental structure.[1] Perplexing as these questions are, I would not have them lead to despair and inaction. The valley authority, or some comparable areal attack on multipurpose development and control of water resources, offers great promise of improved living standards for the whole people. Mechanistic difficulties of an administrative nature must be accepted as challenges to our administrative acumen, not as absolute bars to the realization of the promise of American life.

2

Coördination of Federal activities in the planning and development of resources is not just a government-wide, interdepartmental problem. It is also an intra-departmental concern of such predominantly resource agencies as the Department of the Interior and the Department of Agriculture. The Department of the Interior may be taken as an example of a resource agency currently exploring the possibilities of unifying field service areas and headquarters cities, decentralizing authority,

---

[1] Among the most useful examinations of the valley authority problem are: David E. Lilienthal, *TVA: Democracy on the March* (New York: Harper, 1944); C. Herman Pritchett, *The Tennessee Valley Authority* (Chapel Hill: University of North Carolina Press, 1943); Herman Finer, *The T.V.A.: Lessons for International Application* (Montreal: International Labour Office, 1944); Charles McKinley, "Federal Field Integration and the Valley Authority," *Public Administration Review*, VI (Autumn 1946), 375-384; William Pincus, "Shall We Have More TVA's?" *Public Administration Review*, V (Spring 1945), 148-152; C. Herman Pritchett, "The Transplantability of the TVA," *Iowa Law Review*, XXXII (January 1947), 327-338; Henry C. Hart, "Valley Development and Valley Administration in the Missouri Basin," *Public Administration Review*, VIII (Winter 1948), 1-11.

and providing department-wide area coördination. The objectives of this exploration are to improve program planning, increase administrative economy, and provide better service to the public. The preliminary work in this field was undertaken in the Spring of 1946 by the Department's Coördination Committee at Washington and by temporary field committees in seven cities. A more direct attack was made in September 1946 when Secretary Krug established a permanent Pacific Northwest Coördination Committee, composed of the ranking resident official in this area from each of the eight major agencies of the Department: the Bonneville Power Administration, the Office of Indian Affairs, the Bureau of Land Management, the Bureau of Mines, the Bureau of Reclamation, the Fish and Wildlife Service, the Geological Survey, and the National Park Service. The initial difficulty of defining the Pacific Northwest area was resolved by describing it as the states of Washington, Oregon, and Idaho, and, in connection with water, power, and mineral programs, the additional area of western Montana. Thus, group-of-states regions and natural physical regions were reconciled through resort to the flexible-boundary formula. The Committee is assisted by a small but exceptionally well-qualified staff.

The Pacific Northwest Coördination Committee was directed to prepare recommendations on the scope, adequacy, conflict, and duplication of the Interior Department programs in the area; on the procedures desirable for interchange of information and for formulation and support of a unified departmental program; on an actually integrated areal program for the succeeding fiscal year; on regional organization of the Department in the Pacific Northwest; and on adequacy of delegations of authority by bureaus to their field officials in the area.

Recommendations on some of these matters have already been made, and demonstrate a mature awareness both of the desirability of areal coördination and of the problems in practical arrangements for such coördination among bureaus in the process of being budged out of a traditionally autonomous status. Among those problems are the exceptional centralization of the staff-type, scientific bureaus—the Geological Survey and the Bureau of Mines; the indisposition of these agencies to abandon separate regional schemes for each of their principal functions; the difficulty of accepting as a departmental region the Pacific Northwest west of the Continental Divide, because some agencies need to coöperate with states as distinct jurisdictional units, and because a natural mineral area spans the Rocky Mountains instead of falling exclusively west of the mountain crests; the fact that placing of all agency headquarters at Portland would conflict with each agency's need to place its ranking regional official close to the heart of his region's workload, which varies in geographic incidence from one agency to another; and, perhaps most important, the great variation in patterns of delegation of authority to field officials.

Many of these problems can be solved if there is a firm determination to undertake what the Pacific Northwest Coördination Committee envisions as "an integral attack on the goal of a sustained maximum yield for all the natural resources for which the Department has responsibility."[2] For example, adoption of the flexible-boundary concept would overcome difficulties in realizing substantial identity of regional boundaries. Portland can become a coördination center even if regional officials of some bureaus need to travel there for monthly meetings, or even if they need to appoint liaison officers to serve at Portland with broad powers to commit their bureaus. Persistent effort could force adequate decentralization of authority to regional officials by all bureaus except, possibly, the Geological Survey and the Bureau of Mines. This is the prime requirement for effective areal coördination. At present, many inter-bureau agreements at the regional level are meaningless either because the regional officials have no authority to plan and program their bureau's work in the region, or because that authority is not implemented by adequate authority to shift funds or employ additional personnel so that each partner can perform his agreed share of the joint project. If managerial questions of this type need to be referred to Washington, the whole negotiation may be reopened between agencies at the capital, where sensitiveness to regional needs may not be acute.

The Pacific Northwest Regional Coördination Committee has already gone beyond the submission of recommendations to the Department's Coördination Commit-

---

2 Pacific Northwest Coördination Committee, U. S. Department of the Interior, *Report on Regionalization of Department of the Interior in Region I, The Pacific Northwest* (mimeographed, February 13, 1947), p. 5. See also the Committee's *Supplemental Report on Coördination: Department of the Interior, Region I, The Pacific Northwest* (mimeographed, May 13, 1947).

tee at Washington, and is itself taking responsibility for on-the-ground coördination of particular departmental concerns. Among these are the development of a western phosphate fertilizer industry, region-wide recreation planning, fish conservation in the design and construction of dams, and acquisition of common office space in Portland for Interior Department bureau offices.

The intra-departmental coördination of the Department of the Interior fits into a larger framework of inter-departmental coöperation in the Pacific Northwest. The Washington-based Federal Inter-agency River Basin Committee consists of representatives of the Federal Power Commission and the Departments of Agriculture, the Interior, and the Army. The Columbia Basin Inter-agency Committee, an offshoot of the national Committee, brings these same agencies together monthly on a regional basis. Similarly, the Bonneville Power Administration has an Advisory Board whose membership is identical with that of the Columbia Basin Inter-agency Committee. We may note in passing the curious fact that until 1946 the Bonneville Advisory Board consisted of Washington officials. The representation was shifted to the regional level in general accord with Secretary Krug's decentralization program.

Areal coördination on a committee basis is not a simple solution. At the inter-agency level multiple committees with interlocking memberships are common. These are supplemented on a wheels-within-wheels basis by such intra-agency devices as the Interior Department's Pacific Northwest Coördination Committee. Even then, we have not exhausted the complexities. There remains the problem of regional intergovernmental coöperation, bringing Federal, state, and local officials into concert. Beyond that is the problem of formally enlisting the advisory assistance and support of private citizens who are leaders in the various activities of the region—an important method of tapping the grass roots. Finally, there is the problem of competing geographical bases for coördination. The Pacific Northwest regional coördinating committees, for example, must somehow adjust themselves to such different concepts of the region as that which underlies the Pacific Coast Board of Intergovernmental Relations. They need also to articulate their regional level work with intergovernmental and inter-agency coordination that is at the state, county, and city levels.

3

Experiments in areal coördination are in progress in the Missouri Valley. While these experiments parallel somewhat the current coördination program in the Pacific Northwest, they have a peculiar setting. More than in the Pacific Northwest the inter-agency coördination approach has been a marriage of convenience dictated by the threat of establishment of a valley authority. The Missouri Valley is much larger than the Pacific Northwest, and uncomfortably embraces many more antagonistic interests, which are often sectionalized within the Valley. The Missouri Valley governments and people seem fearful of Federal carpetbagging, and so approach intergovernmental coöperation with suspicion. These and other factors make the setting less promising for areal coördination than is the case in the Pacific Northwest.

I shall describe only sketchily the coördination activities in the Missouri Valley. Many of them take as their starting point the Pick-Sloan plan for development of the Missouri, which is regarded in some quarters as an internally inconsistent merging of the separately prepared plans of the Corps of Engineers and the Bureau of Reclamation. The Missouri Basin Inter-agency Committee, again an offshoot of the Federal Inter-agency River Basin Committee at Washington, brings several Federal agencies together on a regional basis. Sitting with this Basin Committee are five of the ten governors of the area. The Secretary of the Interior also organized, in May 1946, an Interior Missouri Basin Field Committee, charged with coördinative responsibilities and supported by a Reports Staff. Through monthly meetings and staff work, the Committee has addressed itself to the interlocking concerns of its seven member agencies in the conservation of land and water, power production, recreational development, preservation and propagation of fish and wildlife, development of mineral resources, and development of the resources of the Indians. Joint attention to availability of funds, actual expenditures, and physical progress on specific projects under the several agencies' jurisdictions has resulted in joint monthly progress reports from the Missouri Basin Field Committee to the Secretary of the Interior and his Water Resources Committee. A distinctive feature of these reports is the inclusion of state-by-state summaries of progress and problems, prepared by governors or other state officials.[3]

While the initial efforts of the Department of the Interior to achieve areal coördination command our attention here because of their novelty, I do not want to ignore the persistent pressing toward the same goal by the Department of Agriculture. More than with other agencies the Department of Agriculture's internal coördination problem is complicated by problems of relationship with state and county governmental agencies, with a specific clientele, and with segments of that clientele organized in separate associations. An answer to the need for coördination at the state and county levels of many agricultural activities might appear at hand through the State Extension Service and its county agents, who are Federal-state-county officials. The answer is not this simple, for these instrumentalities have traditionally been channels for information, demonstration, and advice, but not for regulation and control, and in some states these instrumentalities are dominated by the American Farm Bureau Federation, which is only one of several farm organizations.[4]

3Areal coördination in the Missouri Valley is masterfully treated in Henry C. Hart, "Valley Development and Valley Administration in the Missouri Basin," *Public Administration Review*, VIII (Winter 1948), 1-11.

4 These problems have been explored in Gladys Baker, *The County Agent* (Chicago: University of Chicago Press, 1939), and John A. Vieg, "Working Relationships in Governmental Agricultural Programs," *Public Administration Review*, I (Winter 1941), pp. 141-148. Note the statement of James G. Patton, President of the National Farmers Union, in a press release of April 14, 1948, on a proposed shift of Soil Conservation Service functions to the Extension Service: "Since we believe deeply that the Extension Service

For our purposes note needs to be made principally of the organization since late 1945 of state and county USDA councils, composed of the heads of state or local offices of constituent agencies of the Department of Agriculture. Each state council also includes the directors of the State Extension Service, the State Experiment Station, and other interested state agricultural agencies. Although the councils are intended to be primarily media for the exchange of information, the discussion of problems of mutual interest, and the promotion of a spirit of coöperation, they are free to make recommendations directly to the Secretary of Agriculture and may be used by the Secretary for the carrying out of specific assignments. In 1946, for example, the Secretary gave them a role in the Emergency Food Program for famine relief. Their other distinctive assignments have been in the study and approval of production goals and the effective communication of production goals to farmers. The USDA councils are clearly but a rudimentary instrument of areal coördination. Whether they can develop into something more significant will depend upon the support they receive from the Secretary, the development of a departmental consciousness among the units in the Department

should confine itself to its original function of education pure and simple, we must oppose this attempt to involve it further with federal action programs. * * * Finally, it is well known that a single farm organization, the American Farm Bureau Federation has sponsored this current campaign to push the Extension Service into another operating field. . . In many states, the Extension Service has been forced into the position of errand boy for this private farm organization. I do not believe this is a healthy condition and we earnestly hope that Congress not only will reject this present attempt at expanding the public funds and personnel available to the Farm Bureau but that it will take steps to end the existing relationship."

of Agriculture, and the resolving of some of the more acute jealousies between the Department and the state and county governments' agricultural agencies.[5]

4

The other two instances of new approaches to areal coördination are geared to intergovernmental coöperation rather than primarily to unification of Federal agency activities. The first of these instances chooses the region as its area. The second is based on individual counties.

The Pacific Coast Board of Intergovernmental Relations, organized in 1945, has 71 members, roughly half representing state and local agencies and half Federal agencies active in the three Pacific Coast states: Washington, Oregon, and California. Quarterly meetings are held under the chairmanship of the governor of the host state, and a small staff serves the Board. The Board focuses on the joint discussion of problems rather than the passing of formal resolutions. Any consensus that may develop depends for implementation on independent actions taken through the separate administrative channels of Federal, state, and local governments. A catalogue of the subjects to which the Board has given attention ranges all the way from housing, public works, and sur-

[5] The organization and activities of the USDA councils are covered by the Secretary of Agriculture's Memorandum No. 1132, October 26, 1945, and the USDA Council Memorandum series issued by the Policy and Program Committee, Office of the Secretary of Agriculture. For the Department's field coördination problem in general, especially at regional centers, consult David B. Truman, *Administrative Decentralization* (Chicago: University of Chicago Press, 1940).

plus property disposal to taxation, welfare costs, and ocean fishing. In addition, the Board has been advised of basic economic trends, covering such problems as population, inflation, and employment as they affect the Pacific Coast. The program is too new for definitive appraisal. Certainly, though, it promotes an understanding among all agencies of the role each plays in the region. It educates them on the character and factual background of problems that cannot be neatly segregated for assignment to a single agency or even a single level of government. And it promotes that informal acquaintanceship among officials without which two-way coöperation cannot readily advance.

While the Pacific Coast Board of Intergovernmental Relations fosters coöperation in a large region, the Federal Council on Intergovernmental Relations has inaugurated experiments in intergovernmental coöperation based on county areas. In five counties, one each in Minnesota, Indiana, Georgia, California, and Washington, county councils on intergovernmental relations have been operating for two to three years. With about a dozen members, most of them private citizens, each council has been engaged in educating itself as to what governmental agencies serve its county area; how their activities mesh together, duplicate, or conflict; and how in some one or few functional fields the obstacles to effective coöperation can be removed. When the county councils need assistance at higher levels, for instance to liberalize delegations of authority to state or Federal field agents in the county, they may turn to the State Council on Intergovernmental Relations, which includes state administrative officials and occasionally local officials and private citizens, and to the Federal Council on Intergovernmental Relations, which includes three top Federal officials, the executive directors of the Council of State Governments and the American Municipal Association, and two political scientists.

As each county council has followed its own bent, a generalized comment on the work of the councils is difficult. However, a few common threads are identifiable. One is the vitality and staying power of these citizen groups' interest in gearing government, however complex, to effective service of the community. Another is the initial assumption of each council that the principal vice was centralization of authority in Federal and state governments and the easy cure the return of authority to local governments. With this must be linked the arrival of each council at a mature appreciation of the validity of Federal and state occupancy of many subject-matter fields; appreciation of the incompetence with which their own local governments were discharging even their existing tasks, partly because of the smallness of local government areas, partly because of the proliferation of units of local government serving the same general area, and partly because local governments were in some instances less responsive to the people than Federal and state agencies; and appreciation of the failure of their local governments to avail themselves of the technical advice and assistance offered by Federal and state governments. Yet another common thread is each council's tendency to find in planning—whether of public works, civic centers, or natural resources—the most fruitful field for intergovernmental coöperation. The councils share, too, a wish for common housing of functionally related agencies and for other devices to provide "one-stop service" for citizens affected by a particular bundle of government functions. What a change in attitude much of this work has meant for council members is best summarized in Rowland Egger's words: "Most of the members of the local councils would agree that the primary function of the local councils on intergovernmental coöperation is to put in motion the forces for cleaning up and modernizing local government, so that local administrative facilities may become effective recipients of delegated state and federal activities."[6]

5

These current experiments demonstrate that the reciprocal adjustment of function and area is of such

[6] John O. Walker, et al., Grass Roots: A Report and an Evaluation (Washington: Council on Intergovernmental Relations, September 1947), p. 50. See also: Blue Earth County Council on Intergovernmental Relations, Democracy Trains its Microscope on Government in Blue Earth County, Minnesota (Mankato, Minn.: Council on Intergovernmental Relations, 1945), and A Study of Public Health Administration in Blue Earth County, Minnesota (Mankato, Minn.; Council on Intergovernmental Relations, undated); T. Hamp McGibony, Governmental Co-operation in Greene County, Georgia (Washington: Council on Intergovernmental Relations, 1945); Henry County Council on Intergovernmental Relations, Adventure in Governmental Gearing in Henry County, Indiana, U.S.A. (New Castle, Ind.: Council on Intergovernmental Relations, 1946); Colquitt County Council on Intergovernmental Relations, Colquitt County, Georgia—A Field Laboratory for Study and Experiment in Intergovernmental Relations (Moultrie, Georgia: Colquitt County Council on Intergovernmental Relations, 1947); Santa Clara County Council on Intergovernmental Relations, A Practical Basis for Developing Better Intergovernmental Relations (San Jose, Calif.: Council on Intergovernmental Relations, 1947). The program of the Federal Council on Intergovernmental Relations was suspended in April, 1948, because of lack of finances.

pressing concern as to be absorbing energies that many functional officials and private citizens would ordinarily prefer to confine to their central occupational concerns. They reveal, too, something of the range of methods of achieving such an adjustment. We may truly unify functions in a region by resorting to the valley authority device. We may coördinate in each area the bureaus of a single Federal department, through committees authorized to make recommendations and joint progress reports to Washington, and to settle some common problems on the spot. We may develop inter-agency coöperation among Federal departments through regional committees. We may seek intergovernmental coöperation through regional committees made up of Federal, state, and local officials. And, at the local level, we may turn to citizen committees for the stimulation of intergovernmental coöperation and the strengthening of the weakest level of government.

I particularly wish to invite students of government to prepare the careful case studies of these experiments that we so greatly need. Here are various approaches to the adjustment of function and area. But what are the conditions for success of each approach? What purposes does each serve best? Are there lessons that are transferable to other forms of areal coördination? Do we know enough about coöperative endeavor in social groups generally to apply this knowledge to the governmental process?

Progress in the science of administration must build on the description and appraisal of particular bodies of administrative experience. Without the solid grounding of case studies, generalization becomes mere opinion. And without reliable generalization there can be no science.

VI: THE RECONCILIATION
OF FUNCTION AND AREA

We have examined the relation of natural physical, social, and economic areas to administrative areas. Administrative areas, we have found, fall into two types: governmental areas, in each of which a general or special unit of government collects funds and administers several functions or a single function; and field service areas, each of which is only a portion of the total area within which a department or bureau of a general government administers its functions. The fact that governmental areas rarely satisfy ideal specifications leads to the need for redrafting of governmental boundaries, horizontal coöperation among contiguous governmental areas, and redistribution of functions and vertical coöperation among the several levels of government. Field service areal patterns for individual functions pose the problem of selecting areas and headquarters cities that conform to dictates of natural areas and administrative efficiency. They also create a setting for consideration of decentralization of administrative authority. Departmental clusters of functions and the totality of functions of a government require that field service areas be geared not only to a single function but to coördinated management of functions in a common area. The clash between functional and areal lines of authority tests the administrative statesmanship of government departments and of the chief executive himself. Current experiments in areal coördination of departmental and governmental activities in a common area suggest new and promising approaches to the reciprocal adjustment of area and function.

There are two ways to reconcile function and area. One is by basic structural reform. The other is by perfecting coöperative techniques. The degree to which progress is made by one of these methods proportionately reduces the pressure on the other. Inter-areal, inter-functional, and inter-level coöperation ameliorates the awkwardness of governmental structural arrangements. To the extent that structure is improved, coöperation need carry less of the load of making government work.

Reconciliation of function and area through the regular machinery of government can take place only if we are clear on certain basic issues. Throughout American life there has developed an emphasis on specialization, segmentation, functional autonomy, and pluralism. It is reflected in education, in professional guildism, and in government, and it finds its epitome in modern industry. In government this emphasis has been expressed in the establishment of relatively independent and autonomous commissions, boards, corporations, code authorities, departments, and special units of government. It less obviously motivates the efforts of administrative bureaus and divisions to win immunity from effective control by department heads and the legislature. This they do through close alliance with interest groups, specialized legislative committees, and independent sources of political support.   These developments threaten to carry functional specialization beyond the point of maximum returns to the people. Persons sharing concern over these and related developments need to devise an architecture that fits the parts into the whole—whether in education, the professions, government, or industry.

In government the architecture of the whole rests on two pillars—major function and area. In any government the many functions and subfunctions can be grouped into a few great clusters for coördinated direction by a top generalist. Through this device the virtues of functional specialization are maintained, but mutual adjustment of the specialties in the light of a major goal of government becomes possible. Those familiar with this device know that functional groupings are never perfect, that such obvious needs as a Federal department of transportation are resisted, that the generalist supervising a cluster of functions may be unable to establish firm control. They know also that, while grouping of functions modifies the extremes to which segmentation and autonomy may go, these clusters themselves are but a part of the whole and may mobilize segmental interests in society in support of programs oriented to those interests.

Area provides the other great foundation for the integration of governmental functions. Area provides the common denominator for the functions of the nation, the state, the county, or the town. Each of these governmental areas has a government that potentially can weave all its functions together so that they make a consistent pattern for the area in which they operate. Similarly, each area of the country, whether a river basin, a group-of-states region, or an existing governmental area like a state or county, provides a common denominator about which can be coördinated all or many field functions of the Federal government.

The problem of area and administration, therefore, is not a minor problem of administrative mechanics worth attention only by administrative technicians. It opens up the fundamental problem of reconciling the parts and the whole, of introducing coherence into an age of specialization, of keeping in view the individual citizen on whom converge the multiple activities of government.

Specialization may be functional or areal. Functional specialization is greatest in higher levels of government and administration. Where a function is performed by Federal, state, and local governments, it is generally true that the Federal agency involved has a galaxy of experts organized in specialized units that cannot be matched in state agencies. Similarly, state agencies in a given functional field tend to be better equipped with specialists than the run-of-the-mill local agencies. Only the great metropolises can match or exceed functional specialization by the states. Moving downward through the hierarchy of governments, then, there is usually a decline in specialization and an increase in generalization. The same observation holds for field service administration. A Federal department mobilizes centrally its highly specialized personnel, while nice distinctions among specialties tend increasingly to vanish through the regional, district, and local levels of the department's field service. In the lowest level of field service areas, the officials are perforce jacks-of-all-trades. This phenomenon, whether in general government or in field administration, can be pictured as a local generalist backed up by a wealth of technical services at the higher levels. A basic problem of administration is to channel these technical services to the local generalist so that he is not snowed under by the volume of reading matter and personal visitations, so that he can distinguish the wheat from the chaff, and so that he is not given conflicting advice or directions on technical matters where his basis for judgment would be inadequate. Much of the future of decentralization rests on our confidence in administration by generalists, our willingness to sacrifice some specialized knowledge at the local or district level, and our minimization of this sacrifice by putting at the area generalists' fingertips the vast range of specialized knowledge available from higher administrative and governmental levels.

Area itself is a basis for specialization and, like functional specialization, can emphasize the parts at the expense of the whole. The introverted nation-state, serving values that have validity only for its portion of the earth's surface, has long obstructed the development of a world structure that would relate the parts to the whole. The coin bearing "regionalism" on its face carries "sectionalism" on its reverse side. States' rights can mask the stake of special interests in feudalistic practices and inequalities of opportunity that are condemned by the nation's conscience. Local areas differ in their orientation toward public policy issues, reflecting the differing social and economic interests of local communities. Even in field administration, each field service area may have a partially different set of problems from the other areas, and its officials may lose sight of the national departmental policy because of their sympathy with the interests of the particular area. If, for example, materials or manpower are to be allocated by field service area officials out of a national pool, there is danger of a competitive race to lower standards so as to get more than the fair portion for one's own field service area. Areal specialization is greatest at the lower levels in the governmental and administrative hierarchy, while the many competing particularisms tend to dissolve into greater generalization at the higher levels.

2

The emergent picture is of a tendency toward functional specialization and areal generalization at the higher governmental and administrative levels, and a tendency toward functional generalization and areal specialization at the lower levels. The fitting of functional parts into the whole of the governmental and administrative process might be expected to occur at the lower levels of government. The fitting of areal particularisms into the whole of national and state policies or departmental policies might be expected to be the task of the higher levels of government and administration. In a sense, it would appear that functions must draw together and abandon some of the niceties of specialization when brought face to face with the ordinary citizen in his local setting, and that areas must draw together and drop something of their particularistic approach when brought face to face with the shared objectives of all people in the nation or in the world.

There are legal and practical limits to the realization of these expectations. Lower levels of government and administration are poorly equipped to provide a structural integration of the many functions of Federal, state, and local governments, or even of the functions of, say, the Federal government alone. There is no machinery for continuous Federal-state-local integration of activities in a given area. Instead, the legal separation of the three levels forces emphasis on coöperation as the only cement for their common interests. Similarly, the Federal government has no field machinery with which to integrate fully its many activities in a particular area.

A major obstacle to the further development of intergovernmental and inter-agency functional coördination at lower levels of government is the lack of coördination at the centers of power. We have seen that areal coördination of the functions of a single Federal department must await the strengthening of the generalist department head at Washington. Similarly, the use of counties or cities as cores about which intergovernmental coördination can develop is severely handicapped by their failure to coördinate even their own functions, to expand their areas to sizes appropriate to modern functional demands, or to absorb the plethora of special, semi-autonomous special districts. Areal coördination of functions among governments and among a government's field agents must therefore await the development of adequate coördination within governments and within departments. Meantime, and perhaps indefinitely, the use of smaller areas to force reassessment of the relation of functional specialties to the whole governmental complex will have to proceed through the perfecting of techniques of intergovernmental and interagency coöperation.

Similarly, there are limits to the ability of higher levels of government and administration to modify the worst features of areal particularism. One of the principal obstacles is the assumption that we must choose between two alternatives. We need not choose between a strong Federal government and a strong state government, between absolute centralization and absolute decentralization, between bureaucratic regimentation and local self-government. The vice of such choices is manifold. Despite elaborate and repeated efforts of social scientists to marshal the advantages and disadvantages of each alternative, the choice is bound to be only pseudo-scientific. It forces us back on prejudices, the emotional symbolism of words, and sheer acts of faith. Once the choice between alternative positions has been made, there is set up an unscientific major premise that colors and distorts any attempt to apply scientific methods to the objective facts of governmental functioning. Instead, science is mustered simply to rationalize a foregone conclusion. The either-or approach precludes recognition of the fact that in the United States at least three magnitudes of governmental areas are needed—national, subnational, and local—and that the people have a stake in the efficiency and popular control of the governments at each of these three levels. In a field service the either-or approach neglects the need for finding a middle ground between central responsibility for results and for equitable treatment of all persons on the one hand, and on the other, adjustment of administration to distinct regional and local conditions.   Both in government as a whole and in field administration we need a pragmatic approach that reflects institutional adaptability to space, time, and motion.   The major premise of our thinking must allow for such adaptability.

Another obstacle to modification of areal particularism in its more extreme manifestations is the lack of a concerted effort by any higher level of government to take account of the problems of the lesser areas.   The relation of the states to the Federal government is given continuous study at no single point in the Federal government.   Nor in any state will there be found a point at which the problems of local areas are considered in a methodical, comprehensive fashion.   In fact, the disorderly manner in which higher levels of government have handled their responsibilities toward the lesser areas accounts for much of the difficulty in which the lesser areas find themselves.   This is less true of field administration. Departmental offices of field operations and the corresponding unit in the Bureau of the Budget provide foci for central consideration of the problems of field service areas.

3

Perhaps the most promising opportunity for reduction of areal particularism and achievement of a happy balance between centralization and decentralization lies in the perfecting of machinery for vertical coördination of a single function among several areal layers. Centralization of authority, it is clear, does not necessitate centralization of administration. Broad policy decisions can be made centrally for a vast area, while important but subordinate policy decisions and application of the policies to individual cases can be made at subcenters for smaller areas. Thus, national policies can be formulated to cover problems whose natural areas exceed state government areas or whose substantially diverse treatment would clash with minimal concepts of equality of opportunity. Yet administration may be decentralized either to Federal field service areas or to the states, counties, and cities.

When should the Federal government administer a Federal function through field service areas and when through states and local governments? The gulf between the two alternatives is illustrated by Paul H. Appleby and David E. Lilienthal. Appleby has written:

If a program is Federal and if the responsibility is Federal, the authority should be Federal and the administering bureaucracy should almost always be Federal. Only thus can national purposes be served; only thus can there be popular control; administrative mechanisms not controllable by a Presidentially appointed top executive are not manageable by the people. The ends hoped for through delegation to the states can be and should be sufficiently attained through decentralization that is wholly Federal. To assume that decentralization and delegation to states are one and inseparable is to assume too much.[1]

Lilienthal takes the opposite tack, in these words:

There are of course many instances where the facts appear to support the claim that good administration of national concerns

[1] Paul H. Appleby, *Big Democracy* (New York: Alfred A. Knopf, 1945), pp. 87-88.

cannot be obtained through the co-operation of local agencies. Local politics, ineptitude, lack of interest and experience in public matters and in administration, brazen partisanship, even corruption—all these stand in the way. I am sure these hazards exist. I am sure, for we have encountered most of them in this [Tennessee] valley. But what are the alternatives? Fewer citizens participating in governmental administration. Less and less community responsibility. More federal employees in the field armed with papers to be filled out and sent to Washington for "processing," because only there is "good administration" possible. The progressive atrophy of citizen interest. An ever wider gulf between local communities and national government, between citizens and their vital public concerns. Such are the alternatives.[2]

Decentralization to governmental areas has several disadvantages under particular circumstances. From the areal standpoint, there are certain functions for which the states are too small as administrative areas. Drainage basin development is an example; the Tennessee Valley Authority, which Lilienthal headed, was a wholly Federal instrumentality, not a coöperative state agency operating under a broad Federal statute. From the standpoint of operational technique, decentralization to governmental areas is probably most effective under substantial grant-in-aid programs. The right of the Federal government to withhold or withdraw the grant-in-aid is the principal sanction through which that government can make the states adhere to standards of administrative efficiency and conform to the national policies for the particular function. What is involved is a double factor. The function, because it involves substantial flowing of

2 David E. Lilienthal, *TVA: Democracy on the March* (New York: Harper, 1944), p. 162.

national funds into the state area, is one that the states rather eagerly embrace. And the possibility that the grant may be suspended by Federal administrators protects the Federal government against lack of state conformity to Federal standards and instructions. This double factor in grant-in-aid programs is lacking in non-grant Federal-state programs, in programs where the grant is too small to affect state self-interest, and in grant programs where the Federal standards clash too sharply with state interests and attitudes.

Let me illustrate. OPA rationing was first entrusted to state rationing administrators appointed by the governors. The program was a strictly regulatory and administrative program attracting to each state no Federal funds other than those for administrative expenses. The state governments were not, therefore, "getting anything out of" their participation in the program, save such psychic dividends as one gets from not being by-passed. The Federal government had no effective sanctions against uncoöperative states, for the threat of withholding of Federal funds was hollow, the discontinuance of the rationing program in the state was not conceivable, and substitution in a few states of direct Federal administration would have been awkward and confusing. Partly in recognition of the inadequacies of Federal-state administration, OPA shifted to direct Federal administration, and even the local price and rationing boards, though essentially instruments of the community staffed by volunteers, were not city or state government agencies, but outposts of the Federal administration.

An example of the possible clashing of grant-in-aid

programs with state interests and attitudes is the proposal of the President's Committee on Civil Rights for "the conditioning by Congress of all federal grants-in-aid . . . for any purpose on the absence of discrimination and segregation based on race, color, creed, or national origin."[3] A minority of the Committee pointed out that the anti-segregation phase of this proposal (as distinguished from the anti-discrimination phase) might conflict so directly with state constitutions, laws, and attitudes as to prevent truly national programs in such fields as health, welfare, roads, and education. In such circumstances, the threat to withhold grants may have little effect, and a grant-in-aid program linked with standards that may exclude the states of a particular region cannot be a very satisfactory mechanism for decentralized administration of a function that needs to be performed. On the other hand, there is doubt that even a program administered through Federal field service areas could too directly storm the fort of cherished sectional prejudices.

Much of what I have been saying may appear to endorse direct Federal administration rather than joint Federal-state administration. That is not my object. Federal-state programs are appropriate for those many functions where the Federal government is making up for the fiscal inadequacy of some states by channeling funds to them to maintain national minima; or where the state has legal authority over certain aspects of a function and the merging of this authority with that of the Federal

3 U. S. President's Committee on Civil Rights, *To Secure These Rights* (Washington: U. S. Government Printing Office, 1947), p. 166.

government promises a more integrated administration from the citizen's standpoint; or where local governments have important legal and administrative authority which a state agency is in the best position to mobilize for support of a joint Federal-state program. In the last type of situation, the state's participation may be limited to the passing of enabling legislation, so that what results is a joint Federal-local administrative operation.

There is one final problem to be met before grant-in-aid programs can be satisfactory media for inter-level structural integration for particular functions. That is the problem of distribution of funds under grant programs. The objectives of the whole range of grant-in-aid activities should be to avoid undue distortion of lesser areas' budget and work programs, to distribute funds in part according to need, (thus advancing the equalization of opportunity for citizens), to preserve incentives to local self-help and local initiative, and to avoid perpetuating by subsidy uneconomic units of government. At present this distributive problem is unsolved.

The reconciliation of function and area, we have suggested, can come about in part through basic structural reform. Such an approach is bottomed on the fact that the national, subnational, and local governments must be made satisfactory vessels for those functions or parts of functions that have respectively a predominantly national, sub-national, or local character. Fiscal adequacy, general governmental efficiency, and popular control, though they now weigh heavily, should not be the factors on which allocation of specific functions depends. They merely distort the effort to assign individual functions to the governmental areas that can provide the closest approximations to natural areas for those functions and that are peculiarly in a position to give efficient administration to those functions. To remove from the picture the distorting factors calls for a number of actions.

Basic readjustment of governmental areas is important if we are to have areas that can assure fiscal adequacy and general efficiency and qualify for the discharge of functions that currently fall to higher-level areas only by default. I rule out readjustment of state boundaries, for we are not constructing a utopia. But readjustment of local government areas is urgent, for the smallness of such areas directly accounts for much of the local units' fiscal inadequacy, general inefficiency, and inability to provide able administration of the particular functions appropriate on other grounds for local governments. Readjustment of local areas has traditionally been a matter for local action. Yet in the past generation local action to consolidate counties and annex suburbs to cities has been almost nil. If we are not to continue to see local government wane, the state governments must be induced to establish local areas appropriate to modern needs. True, this is centralization of a sort, and the emotional advocates of local self-government will vehemently protest. But I am convinced that only by decisive state action to provide the areal setting necessary for healthy local government can the real values of decentralization be preserved. A precedent is set by the British establishment in 1945 of a Local Government Boundary Commission, which can recommend to Parliament the moving of municipal boundaries and the consolidation of local government units.[4]

Action to meet the problem of fiscal adequacy must go beyond mere readjustment of governmental areas. Enlargement of such areas will not answer the problem of cities and counties located in economically weak sections. Again the answer seems to be resort to the next higher level of government. Through shared-revenue and grant-in-aid programs the states can backstop the poorer local governments. A vertical relationship designed along fiscal aid lines has overtones of centralization, but seems in its ultimate values to offer promise of strengthening rather than weakening state and local government. It is in many cases the only alternative to wholesale transfer of functions to higher levels of government or toleration of low and disparate standards of government service. Fiscal aid, of course, should not be used, as it sometimes has been, to perpetuate weak local areas that could be strengthened by consolidation with neighboring areas.

[4] Coleman Woodbury, "Britain Begins to Rebuild Her Cities," *American Political Science Review*, XLI (October 1947), 907; Winston W. Crouch, "Trends in British Local Government," *Public Administration Review*, VII (Autumn 1947), 256-57. The drafting of comparable legislation in this country will call for a high order of skill. Incentive to action must be provided (*cf.* legislative inertia on reapportionment of legislative representation), yet the legislature should not be tempted to use its powers in punitive fashion against local areas controlled by rival political parties or factions. An alternative to decisive state action reshaping local areas is state passage of enabling legislation that weights the scales in favor of consolidation and annexation. A state law authorizing local voting on annexation of a suburb by a city can call for merging of the votes cast in the city and the suburb, with the majority of the total determining whether annexation will take place. Contrast this with the customary requirement that the city and the suburb must each separately vote in favor of annexation for it to be consummated.

While assurance of areal and fiscal adequacy should do much to strengthen local units, the general efficiency of such units might be further promoted by state prescription of minimal standards in such matters as budgeting, accounting, debt incurrence, and personnel selection techniques. Here, too, a degree of centralization is advocated in order that decentralization may flourish.

4

It is not my purpose to outline a comprehensive program for strengthening national, state, and local governments. There are impressive bodies of literature on such needs as reform of the whole tax structure, improvement of the organization of the executive branch of each level of government, and strengthening of the machinery for popular control of administration. I shall content myself with a final structural proposal.

Each of the superior levels of government, the states and the Federal government, should give institutional recognition to its interest in aiding the next lower level of government. This interest has to date been segmented so that it flows entirely along functional lines. Each of the superior government's functional agencies—in education, roads, health, public assistance—has administered a distinct program of grants, technical assistance, and control. But neither the state nor the Federal government has organized itself for comprehensive attention to the problems of the next lower level of government. The gap has been filled in part by the Council of State Governments, leagues of municipalities, associations of county commissioners, and similar voluntary organizations. I do not mean to underestimate their contributions, but it is obvious that such groups are often unable to maintain an adequate staff; to approach the superior level of government with objectivity, sympathy, and a minimum of self-interest; or to recommend such apparently suicidal measures as consolidation of local government areas, transfer of functions to a higher level of government, elimination of their own tax sources, wiping out of double taxation and inter-area trade barriers, or application of the merit system of appointment to posts currently filled by election or patronage.

I suggest that the Federal government and each state establish a staff unit on intergovernmental relations, preferably in the executive office of the President or governor, charged with taking an over-all view of at least three problems. One is the vertical relation of its government to the governments at the next lower level. A Federal unit on intergovernmental relations, for example, should certainly be giving attention to the pattern of Federal aid to states that has resulted from the many *ad hoc* decisions by Congress and the executive branch. The impact of Federal taxes on state revenues and of both on the taxpayer; the effect on the state and local governments of Federal acquisition of property for national forests, reservoirs, and Federal office buildings; the possibility of transferring back to the states certain functions that the Federal government earlier acquired; the stimulation of Federal-state coöperation through regional or state boards of intergovernmental relations; the decentralization of administrative authority to Federal field agents so that they can share effectively in areal planning—all illustrate the wealth of problems that need orderly consideration. The possibilities at the state level are even more promising, for under the unitary doctrine of state-local relations the state governments have a peculiarly great impact on local governments.

The second problem to which such a staff unit might give attention is the horizontal relations among the governments at the next lower level. The Federal unit, for instance, would be concerned with interstate trade barriers and double taxation, on both of which the Federal government has means for influencing a reasonable solution. The state unit could do much to encourage areal boundary adjustments, use of inter-area contracts, joint purchasing of equipment and supplies, and other coöperative undertakings.

Finally, a staff unit on intergovernmental relations could channel a wealth of information and advice to aid the lower-level governments in more efficient discharge of their responsibilities. One of the common conclusions of the five county councils on intergovernmental relations has been that local government officials are unaware of the amount of technical assistance that is available from agencies of superior levels of government. This aid could be made known, and the staff unit could itself provide aid on more general problems of governments—such as what the experience of other governments and the appraisals by students of government indicate as the values and, most importantly, the conditions of success of council-manager government, the merit system, and central purchasing. It could socialize knowledge of best tax collection procedures and public reporting techniques. All of these aids could be geared to the peculiar conditions of the area occupied by the staff unit's government. A state staff unit, for instance, while giving due attention to experience throughout the country, could advise within the framework set by the state's constitutional, statutory, and administrative requirements applicable to local governments; and it could emphasize the lessons pointed by the experience of local governments in the particular state, an experience that should carry more weight locally than either the experience in distant states or the generalizations of academes.

There are other problems than these on which a state staff unit could make contributions. For instance, it could concern itself with the state's relations to the Federal government and to other states. I do not stress these, however, for they are not essential to the central concept—that of a unit at a superior level of government that recognizes its government's strategic position for aiding governments at the lower level, and the government's obligation to appraise its own activities as they impinge on the work of the lesser governments.

Action on the proposal can be taken only if two cautions are observed. The unit must be purely staff in function. It gives no orders, it dispenses no grants: it merely advises local governments. It does not supersede or control the functional agencies of its own government, nor does it require that their contacts with local governments be channeled through its facilities. The staff unit, of course, takes over no functions of the chief executive or legislature. Defining a staff function of necessity stresses these negative aspects. But on the positive side, there is great promise of results from an agency that advises smaller governmental areas, advises functional departments at its own level, and advises its chief executive and legislature.

The second caution is that such a staff unit must be staffed with persons in whom the lower levels have confidence. Ideally a state staff unit should be headed by a man who has served in local governments with distinction, and the Federal unit might be headed by a former governor or state budget director. Certainly, because centralization is so facile an answer to our ills, the unit should be dominated by the philosophy of a Lilienthal or a Krug, constantly probing for ways in which authority can be decentralized and, as a prerequisite to that, ways in which the potential recipients of such delegation can be strengthened so that they qualify for the exercise of additional duties.

My advocacy of such a permanent staff unit on intergovernmental relations stems from a conviction that temporary commissions that prepare reports and dissolve have not proven fruitful, that even less successful have been the monographs and textbooks of scholars, and that there are regrettable limitations to the contributions that can be made by voluntary associations of governmental areas and officials. None of these other lines of attack should be or will be abandoned. But we desperately need a new device that has some promise of speeding the improvement of efficiency in all our governments and of strengthening and rationalizing the machinery for inter-functional and inter-areal coördination.

In the Federal government's field administration the following are among the principal structural requirements: Grouping of functions and subfunctions by departments to provide coördinated policy and administration for such major functions as natural resources development, transportation, and welfare; strengthening of departmental generalists at Washington and in field service areas; development of common headquarters cities and office buildings; development of valley authorities and fitting of them into the Federal structure; extension of the Bureau of the Budget's field offices and expansion of the concept of their function; and conversion of postoffices and perhaps county agents into local centers qualified to provide elementary information about Federal activities, to advise citizens as to which agencies or officials should be consulted for help on particular problems, and to distribute government publications of general interest.

5

The fact that no area we define and no functional assignment of any agency can be self-sufficient puts a premium on inter-areal and inter-functional coöperation. We need to know a great deal more than we do about ways in which coöperative techniques can supplement the basic structure of government and administration. For example, can we isolate the several types of coöperation and determine the conditions applicable to each? In the course of our examination of areal problems of administration we have come across a number of types. One is joint sponsorship of research to develop facts and analyses to which all the coöperating agencies will be exposed, and on the basis of which they can exchange views. This is the formula of the Pacific Coast Board of Intergovernmental Relations. Its key feature is that joint decisions are not precipitated, the coöperation stopping with mutual education. Another type of coöperation is joint planning and programming for continuing functions, which underlies regional, state, and local planning commissions, is a key element in the Interior Department's Pacific Northwest Coördination Committee, and has been found by the county councils on intergovernmental relations to be fundamental, practical, and potentially most fruitful. Again, though, the emphasis is on the thinking preceding action, not upon action itself which, if it proceeds at all in accordance with the plans, is the individual responsibility of each agency and not a combined operation. A variant is to link this approach with a system of progress reporting by a central staff, as is done by the Interior Department's Missouri Basin Field Committee. Coöperation can take the form of joint decision of matters that can be settled once and for all. This has been found the most useful objective for interstate compacts. In its most fully developed form, coöperation can become continuing collaboration on such a planning and operations project as the development of the resources of a great river basin. Or, more modestly, coöperation can stress the periodic bringing together of agencies and governments for the regular adjustment of operational inconsistencies and conflicts in carrying functional programs to the people. Provision for pooled housekeeping services and inter-agency clearance of fact-gathering projects, aimed at greater efficiency and economy in a somewhat narrow sense rather than at program coördination and joint functional operations, appears to have dominated the Bureau of the Budget's field offices as it dominated earlier efforts at government-wide areal coördination.

The problem of coöperation raises questions not only about the objectives but also about the machinery of coöperation. For example, what are the respective uses of two-way coöperation between equals, multiple coöperation involving many participants, and coöperation through intervention of a neutral party as mediator? We do know, I believe, that coöperation so diffused in purpose and in participants as to be merely "coöperation in general" has utility only in promoting informal acquaintance among officials and permitting a general pooling of information on agency functions and problems. These create a helpful atmosphere, but they are not coöperation in the literal sense. The most profitable coöperation requires a limited number of participants and limited objectives both of function and of area. Through conferences and committees we may get coöperation among agencies concerned with water resources. But there is little use in bringing such agencies together frequently with agencies building battleships, catching stray dogs, and licensing insurance agents. Multi-functional coöperation has its parallel in multi-areal coöperation. Two-way or regional interstate coöperation has more promise of specific results than efforts to get the 48 states to act in concert on anything more specific than the adoption of resolutions approving proposals "in principle." We need, though, to ask whether there are techniques of representation by which the participants in coöperation may be limited though the functions or areas for which coöperation is sought are numerous. Two examples of this representative principle at work may be cited. A few governors and legislators constituted the Council of State Government's Committee on State-Local relations. On the Pacific Coast Board of Intergovernmental Relations, local areas are represented by officials of municipal leagues and county supervisors' associations. In these cases the results are published reports or simply exchanges of views, rather than decisions on a course of action. Can the representative principle be pressed beyond such limited results, or is it necessary always to bring together authoritative representatives of every unit whose agreement may be necessary to the taking of action?[5] The Missouri Basin Inter-Agency Committee, which in effect includes five governors selected by the ten governors of the area, is one indication that the principle of representation has important potentialities. The question is posed rather acutely even in agencies and governments that the layman assumes are hierarchically organized. Federal departments and state governments, for example, often cannot coöperate with each other through a few representatives with broad functional or areal responsibilities. Instead, the coördinative machinery with-

[5] The Security Council of the United Nations provides an interesting case study of this problem. The major powers, whose agreement is thought necessary to any effective international security action, are authoritatively and individually represented, but the bulk of the nations of the world are represented by non-permanent members of the Council, chosen with an eye to geographic distribution.

in departmental and governmental hierarchies is so loose and unacknowledged that the bureaus within a department and the agencies in a state government may insist that no generalist above them can represent their interests.

Means of preventing frustration of coöperative efforts are needed. Perhaps the readiest cure can be found in situations where the coöperating units have a common superior to whom unresolved disputes can be referred either for decision or for mediative intervention. For example, questions on which the members of the Interior Department's Pacific Northwest Coördination Committee cannot reach agreement are to be referred by the chairman to the Department's Coördination Committee at Washington, with recommendations for consideration by the Secretary of the Interior. This is an easy arrangement in a hierarchically organized Federal department whose generalists have asserted a measure of authority. Can we approach a similar arrangement to facilitate interdepartmental and intergovernmental coöperation? Most coöperative groups work on the absolute veto principle. Can this hurdle be surmounted in certain circumstances by introduction of a different principle? If not a majority or two-thirds principle, would it be useful to explore the utility of the Friends' consensus principle, which might free agencies from formally quibbling over every detail of wording and leave the discovery and statement of a consensus to an able executive secretary or neutral chairman of the group?

The pace of a coöperative group, in which the chairman (if any) is a presider but not a decider, is set by the member least able to commit his agency or least disposed to coöperate. I remind you of the analogy of the United Nations Security Council. The member of an inter-agency committee who is least able to commit his agency will drag the whole committee's work down to his level of possible agreement, or, alternatively, will force the committee to delay its work while he obtains clearance for each agreement up the hierarchy of his agency. In the field service, this means that the pace is fixed by the most centralized agency. So, too, in an intergovern-mental group, the governor with the least authority over his state's administrative agencies, or the county commis-sioner from the most jerry-built county government, will most impede the arrival at agreements. In other words, the least coöperative or least authoritative representative of an agency will fix the least common denominator gov-erning the committee's work. The least common denomi-nator also has areal significance. In a committee whose members speak for dissimilar areal expanses, though cov-ering in part the same ground, agreement will tend to be restricted to the only area common to them all, namely the smallest area to which any agency representative's authority is restricted.

Coöperation often needs a shove from outside. Neith-er agency involved may be willing to take the initiative toward coöperation. In some cases there is a reluctance to propose discussions that might reduce the agency's freedom of action. Perhaps a "convener" in a neutral po-sition might bring the agencies together. A convener can be found in the regular hierarchy of departments. The Bureau of the Budget's field offices could perform this role for interdepartmental problems of the Federal government.[6] But can we devise a comparable convener arrangement to facilitate intergovernmental coöperation? Another way of providing a shove from outside is through citizen groups. The Santa Clara County Council on Intergovernmental Relations found that "public officials are naturally quite reluctant to take the initiative in such matters"[7] and so has served both as a neutral outsider and as a pressure group to stimulate coöperation among governments operating in the county. In cities the community councils composed of representatives of voluntary citizen organizations may well perform a similar function.

A concept expressed in the first lecture has utility for the approach to interareal and interfunctional coöperation. We saw then that in defining a natural area, whether it be a single-factor or a multi-factor area, it is easier to identify the core than to set down a hair-line boundary of the area. We have spoken of fringes and of border zones as more accurate characterizations than "boundaries." Wider acceptance of this distinction will help in dealing with governmental and field service areas. The vague boundary is not, for example, a major obstacle to coöperative planning, as distinguished from operating, activities. It is possible for a plan to be developed among the New England states for the New England region, and

---

[6] Henry C. Hart reports that on the Missouri Basin Inter-Agency Committee "it is the [governors] who, having comprehensive interests in development, and being free from suspicion of bureaucratic wrangling which would embarrass one federal member in publicly cross-examining another, have precipitated the resolution of situations where agencies were working at cross purposes." "Valley Development and Valley Administration in the Missouri Basin," *Public Administration Review* VIII (Winter 1948), 5.

[7] Santa Clara County Council on Intergovernmental Relations, *A Practical Basis for Developing Better Intergovernmental Relations* (San Jose, Calif.: Council on Intergovernmental Relations, 1947), p. 47.

for a plan to be developed for New York City's region. The fact that Connecticut would fall in the border zones of each region does not preclude that state's having a share in the development of both plans. Many a state will find itself astride the ridge between two drainage basins. Yet there is no reason why separate plans for such basins cannot be developed. What is true of planning is also true to some extent of other types of inter-agency and intergovernmental coöperation. The Interior Department may not need to force absolute identity of boundaries on its bureaus to obtain department-wide coördination at a core city like Portland, Oregon. Its water-resource bureaus may include the western part of Montana in their Pacific Northwest field service areas, while its bureaus that deal with state governments may draw the line at Montana's western boundary. Still, Portland-based coöperation for a generally common Pacific Northwest area can proceed. Even the state governments might recognize that their border counties need special enabling legislation so that they can freely coöperate with neighboring counties in adjacent states. City boundaries are often ignored for purposes of extending into the border fringe police and fire protection, subdivision regulation, and zoning. Boundaries of governmental areas and field service areas, in other words, must not be conceived as walls having no chink through which a governmental Pyramus and Thisbe can express their coöperative spirit.

The central mechanism for coöperation is the committee. We need to know more about the situations when a committee is useful, the conditions of its success, the problems that it brings in its train. For example, all experience indicates that a continuing committee needs a staff. A staff can give the committee a sense of institutional existence and continuity apart from that of the committee members of the represented agencies and governments. It can bring a neutral and comprehensive approach to bear on the committee's assignment, which the committee members representing segments of the subject-matter and representing special viewpoints cannot provide. It can restrict the potential area of disagreement by providing a factual framework within which committee discussion may proceed.

Again, study of a group of committees might reveal problems of intercommittee coöperation when several committees are concerned with related functions or areas. We have earlier noted the multiplication of intergovernmental and interagency committees in the Pacific Northwest. This creates interfunctional coöperation problems. We have noted also the overlapping of Pacific Northwest committees with Pacific Coast committees. This creates inter-area coöperation problems. Sometimes intercommittee coöperation can be provided by identical membership for separate committees, as with the Bonneville Advisory Board and the Columbia Basin Interagency Committee. Another possibility is for the Bureau of Budget field office to provide a central secretariat serving all major interdepartmental (and, possibly, intergovernmental) committees in particular areas. Thus committees could be discreetly brought to an awareness of common interests and intercommittee coöperation could be stimulated, much as has been done in some agencies at Washington having a galaxy of policy committees served by a central secretariat.

My purpose is not to dispose of the problem of coöperation, but to stimulate further thinking about a phase of government that has been inadequately explored despite its fundamental importance for public administration. We need to know more about the objectives, the machinery, and the dynamics of coöperation, for coöperative methods ameliorate the rigidities and unsolved problems of the basic administrative structure.

Our review of the opportunities for reconciling function and area through basic structural reform and through development of coöperative techniques reveals the tasks still to be accomplished in the fields of research and action. The former I have tried to acknowledge through the suggestion of many problems on which we need case studies and penetrating thought. I should not wish to modify what I have already said on that score. It is abundantly evident, however, that an even more crucial need is the building of a bridge across the chasm between research in the social sciences and action in the arena of everyday affairs. We already have a vast fund of scholarly studies on problems of areal administration. These are read mostly by other scholars and their findings are synthesized only in textbooks addressed to undergraduate students. We need to explore techniques for bringing research findings into the mainstream of social action. One device is suggested by the example of the Council of State Governments' Committee on State-Local Relations. Here 10 officials from different states, including governors and legislators, formed a committee, were aided by a research staff and technical consultants, and agreed on a report that distills the findings of scores of research studies on state-local relations. A synthesis sponsored by practical men of government and addressed to their colleagues may well be a major means of speeding the translation of experts' recommendations into practical applications.

Another approach is that exemplified by the Southern Regional Training Program in Public Administration. It seeks to develop one type of social science technician, described by Pendleton Herring as "an individual who has been professionally trained to apply to practical situations the facts, generalizations, principles, rules, laws, or formulae uncovered by social science research." This requires not only knowledge of a social science discipline, but "those intangible skills that are the product of both personality and successful experience. Judgment, common sense, and a sharp eye for relevancy are part of the necessary equipment."[8] The flow into government of technicians trained by the combined resources of the Universities of Alabama, Kentucky, and Tennessee, familiar with the body of research on areal problems of administration, and skilled in the application of such research to practical situations, may well be a major phase of the strategy of action that we so acutely need.

6

Reviewing our path in this final lecture, we have discovered that function and area can be reconciled by a

[8] Pendleton Herring, "The Social Sciences in Modern Society," in Social Science Research Council, *Items*, I (March 1947), 5.

combination of structural reform and perfection of coöperative techniques. Structural reform has as one of its principal objectives the realizing of the advantages of functional and areal specialization without sacrifice of that constant relating of the parts to the whole without which government becomes an anarchic chaos. A major need is for higher level governments controlling large areas to create those conditions in whose absence lower level governments concerned with lesser areas will be unable to exercise their appropriate functions. Similarly, each government and each department of the major governments need to provide sufficient functional coördination by generalists to make functional specialization serve the larger goals of democracy. We have rejected the dichotomous approach to the problem of centralization. By way of example, some of the conditions that determine when Federal functions should be administered through the Federal field service and when through state and local governments were outlined. The most critical truly areal problem exists at the local government level. Our failure to solve this and related problems of local government is more responsible for centralist tendencies than any hunger for power on the part of Federal and state officials. Nevertheless, part of the blame for the local situation rests with the disorderly handling of Federal and state responsibilities for activities that impinge on local areas. One remedy is the establishment by the Federal government and by each state government of a staff office of intergovernmental relations, so that there can be a continuous appraisal of the implications of higher level decisions and practices on the health of local areas.

Coöperation is the interstitial cement of inter-functional, inter-level, and inter-areal relations. We examined in preliminary fashion some of the objectives and devices for coöperation, primarily with a view to inviting further exploration of this important practical phase of administration. Attention was called to the need for a bridge between research and action in the reconciliation of function and area.

Concluding, I would urge that we recognize that area and function will be reciprocally adjusted not by a single solution but by many, and that the adjustment is a continuous and imperfect process, not one to be realized once and for all. It is easy to call for a single uniform pattern of field service areas or for constitutional home rule for cities or for higher governments to act as receivers in bankruptcy for lower-level governments. It is easy to be impatient at the great gaps between experts' recommendations and the reforms actually instituted. Lest we despair too easily, let me remind you that the published literature on field service areas is only a dozen years old, that many of the voluntary organizations for intergovernmental coöperation are even younger, and that we have barely begun to associate experts on areal problems with strategic centers of decision-making in government and with intergovernmental commissions, committees of public officials, and citizen groups specifically concerned with areal coördination of governmental functions. No foreign federal government has found the perfect answer to Federal-state relations. No unitary government is without criticism for its relations with local units. No nation's local governments and areas are without archaic features or immune from the trend toward centralization.

INDEX